REDEFINING
NORMAL

AN OPEN INVITATION
FOR ORDINARY PEOPLE
WANTING TO BECOME
EXTRAORDINARY DISCIPLES

dave rhodes

© 2011 by Wayfarer

Printed by Keys Printing, Greenville, S.C.

Written by: David Rhodes
@dave_rhodes

Art direction: Blake Berg
Graphic designer: Pete Berg
Editor: Robert Neely

Wayfarer
www.wayfarer.tv

3DM
PO Box 719
Pawleys Island, SC 29685
www.weare3dm.com

ISBN: 978-0-615-52319-4

Table of Contents

"Dave Rhodes is one of the most gifted and powerful communicators I've ever partnered with, and I've been waiting for this book for years! He has profoundly impacted my life and ministry; I'm certain it'll be the same for you."

Aaron Keyes, Worship Pastor, Grace Fellowship, Atlanta, Georgia

"Since I met Dave Rhodes more than 15 years ago, he has always been about creating experiences for people to view God and interact with him differently than they have for most of their life. His new book Redefining Normal is no different. It is a great encouragement for all Christ followers in all shapes and sizes to move from being hearers of the Word to doers. I highly recommend that you don't just read the book but instead accept the invitation and step into the life intended for you."

Roger Davis, President, Student Life, Birmingham, Alabama

"I've never been more challenged to break the mold of normality in pursuit of the heart and mission of God. As a friend of Dave's for many years, I'm grateful for his honesty and diligence to speak truth to our culture that often settles for the mundane, while God invites us into a brilliant and daring adventure with Him. I'm excited to bring my team at The Austin Stone into this conversation that Dave has started in Redefining Normal."

Aaron Ivey, Pastor of Worship, The Austin Stone Community Church, Austin, Texas

"Finally, a book for the church that's not about the church, but about discipleship. Dave helps readers engage in practical ways to let Jesus disciple you and then challenges you to get in on discipling others. Full of witty and engaging personal illustrations as well as practical tools, this book is sure to be a refreshing read for anyone serious about following Christ and impacting others."

Brandon Schaefer, Follow Jesus Pastor, Southland Christian Church,
Lexington, Kentucky

"I am thrilled that my friend Dave Rhodes has finally written down what he has lived over the last couple of decades. His words are a prophetic fire that smolder across the pages — words that inspire and disturb me. I am inspired about creating a discipleship culture in our churches; disturbed by what we have substituted for it. Thank you, Dave, for not talking about problems, but offering solutions; for not just tearing down, but building up; and for being deeply theological but also accessible."

Chris Brooks, Pastor and teacher, The Well, Tuscaloosa, Alabama

"Dave's new book has forever rocked my world! He has a fresh understanding of discipleship that makes so much sense in a complicated religious world. I've known Dave for many years, and in a world of Christian hype, Dave is quite frankly down-to-earth, authentic, and is wise beyond his years. If you only read one book on making disciples, I think this is the one!"

Steve Keyes, Founding Pastor, CrossRoads Community Church, Greenville, S.C.

"I think that Dave has thrown a strike right down the middle here. Dave is asking us to redefine when it comes to normal Christianity. He's inviting us not to hold Christ off at a distance an see if we measure up to him, but to hold him so close to us that there is no separation between Christ and us. Thanks, Dave, for this fresh vision of what my relationship with Christ could look like."

Rob Castle, Event Director, Momentum Student Conference, Hickory, N.C.

"I'm a fan of Dave Rhodes! I love his heart for God and his passion to make disciples. This book calls the church back to basics in a fresh way. Read it and you'll think differently, more deeply, about how God is calling you live in his story as a follower of Jesus."

Charlie Boyd, Directional Leader and Teaching Pastor, Southside Fellowship,
Greenville, S.C.

"Redefining Normal will challenge you to examine the mediocrity in your own spiritual life. I recommend you read the book slowly and ask yourself if you are following Jesus' command to make disciples or just playing at church."

Bill Hughes, Minister to Students and Singles, First Baptist Church, Tifton, Georgia

"Redefining Normal is a very thought-provoking and practical guide to Christian discipleship. Dave is not only a very gifted thinker; he is also able to communicate spiritual truths in a clear and useful way. This book challenges the status quo of 'business as usual' discipleship and helps to direct Christ followers to dream what life could be like in a transformed world."

Greg Allgood, Director of Campus Ministries, Anderson University, Anderson, S.C.

"It is one thing to think about God; it is another thing to think about God accurately. Dave Rhodes is a master at creating conversations that help us think rightly about God. The church needs a richly pragmatic and deeply stirring book on spiritual formation, and Redefining Normal is a great place to start!"

Ryan Britt, Director of Global Missions, 12Stone Church, Lawrenceville, Georgia

SECTION
ONE

The Call

*T*here is a difference between religion and faith. Religion tells stories; faith has a story to tell.

This book is an invitation to reclaim the life of faith from inside the religion of Christianity. But more than that, it is an invitation for you to actually become a person of faith yourself. This life of faith is different than a set of beliefs or behaviors. The reason is that, before faith is either of those things, it is first a dynamic interaction with a person — a person to be followed. And sometimes the faith journey of following this person we call Christ puts you at odds with the religion that bears his name.

Allow me to explain.

I want to follow Christ. In some ways this is something that I have wanted as long as I can remember. But this is not something I came to by myself. I grew up in a Christian home with unbelievable parents and a thoughtful and passionate younger brother, surrounded by an extended family of mentors and friends. God-following was what brought us together. God-following was what united our struggles and unleashed our celebration. We weren't always right in our thinking about who God is or how God is. We didn't always live out our faith identity with the integrity we desired. But we knew who we were seeking, and we knew something about him was calling us to change. And so we did. Because we did, other things changed as well. Some things changed in us. Other things changed around us. We were not who we were when we started this journey. And at some point the change leaked out — which was and is pretty much the point.

Now, just because on my best days I have the audacity to call myself Christ's disciple doesn't mean I have gotten there overnight or without difficulty. In fact, it doesn't even mean that I have arrived. Just talking with the kind of language that makes it seem as though I have arrived makes me cringe. For me, this whole faith thing remains much more of a journey than a destination. I'm becoming a disciple as much as I am one. And much of this journey has been accompanied with tension. Not just tension inside myself, but the deep tension that I have noticed between following Christ and fitting in to Christianity.

Even though my life is a testimony to the tens and hundreds of Christians within the church who have invested Christ's life in me, for me growing in Christ has come at the cost of moving against the grain of the Christian system and subculture. It has kept me from really feeling like I could buy off on or leap into the system. And this is not because I'm a rebel. Anyone who knows me well would tell you that rebellion doesn't come naturally to me. It's just that the more closely I watch Jesus, the more a dichotomy has risen in my spirit between what is and what should be. This tension raises its head almost every day that I have tried to follow after Jesus. I cannot help but feel a strain between Christ and Christianity.

Over the past 10 years, as I've begun to voice this dichotomy and dissatisfaction aloud, first with cautious timidity and now with a little calculated boldness, I've also noticed how much this tension resonates with others.

There seems to be a restlessness just below the surface inside Christianity today not unlike the restlessness of other marquee moments in our Christian heritage. It's a restlessness of what everyone knows but is afraid to say out loud. (Even typing the following words feels a little heretical to me.) Christ and Christianity have become two different things. And trying to fit into the Christian system on one hand and trying to follow Christ on the other hand can be exhausting — physically, emotionally, mentally, relationally, and spiritually. As a result, too often instead of addressing this tension, Christians find it easier to just give in to the system and settle for the status quo.

Not anymore.

It's time to Redefine Normal.

I'm convinced we cannot always both follow Christ and fit into Christianity. Sometimes following the person means redefining the system. In fact, sometimes if we don't redefine the system, the system will confine the person.

In the end, one will eventually trump the other. And so I'm doing my best to choose Christ. I'm letting Christ redefine my Christianity.

It's at this point that I need to say just as boldly that I am not against the church. I love the church. My aim is not to simply destroy or deconstruct the church or those in it. I myself am one of those in it. But my goal is to recall the church. This is not my way of calling the church to be what I want it to be. Instead, I hope to recall it back to what it was always supposed to be. I want to be one voice among many that are unleashing the subversive revolution of Christ-following back into the church one heart at a time.

This is why I am writing this book. My hope is that those who read it become the church. My hope is that you will join the revolution. My hope is that, as in so many other times in our Christian heritage, reformation and revival will lead to something new — not just in our lives personally but also in our systems. My hope is that we will change, and that as we change, everything else will change too. My hope is that, for some, this book may actually Redefine Normal.

So here is my open invitation to you: You may feel like an ordinary person, but you can become an extraordinary disciple. You too can change the world. And if enough of us do, we can Redefine Normal not just in our lives but everywhere.

CHAPTER
ONE

Toy Soldiers

"There are, in the end, only two ways open to us —
to honestly and honorably make an admission of how far we are
from the Christianity of the New Testament, or to perform skillful tricks
to conceal the true situation." — **Soren Kierkegaard**

"Then Jesus came to them
and said, 'All authority in heaven
and on earth has been given to me.
Therefore go and make disciples...'"
—Matthew 28:18-19a

*O*ne of the first illustrations that I developed as a speaker is one that I still tell today. I tell it to kids and adults. Both seem to get it. This illustration follows me around and has become part of my speaking folklore. And through this illustration, I first stumbled upon the truth this book is all about. So I want to tell it again to begin our journey.

I love my mom and dad. They were great parents. But one of the things that I remember most about growing up was that they constantly made me do things that I didn't understand. Crazy things like making my bed. Didn't they know that I was just going to get back into it the next night? But every day, it was the same thing: "David, make your bed!" Even on days on which I had managed to go almost the entire day without making my bed, those words would echo through the hallways to my room. Sometimes this happened less than an hour before bedtime. I didn't get it. No one was coming over. No one would see. But there I was, making my bed sometimes even as I was getting into it.

Then there were other things like raking the yard in the middle of the Fall. I didn't get this one either. I always thought we should just rake the yard after all the leaves were off the trees at the end of the Fall. But my dad insisted we rake the yard all throughout the season.

However, the thing that my mom made me do most as a little kid that I never quite understood was going to the grocery store with her. I wanted to stay home with the dog, but there I was: a 6-year-old kid in the frozen food section questioning my existence and what it had to do with going to the grocery store. Now those of you who remember your life taking on a similar trajectory also know that the worst part of going to the grocery store with your mom is that moms don't go to the grocery store like normal people. Most people have a small list and go get what they need. But not moms. Moms walk up and down every aisle of the grocery store, looking at every item, contemplating, weighing, budgeting, and deciding whether or not they need it for the week. I remember walking up aisle one and down aisle two. We walked up aisle three and down four. On and on it went. We walked slowly and methodically. And all the while, I had no idea why I needed to be there.

But then, on aisle nine, I found my reason for being at the grocery store. Around aisle nine of every grocery store is something called the cereal aisle. And on this aisle, my mom turned to me and said, "OK, David, it's your turn. Pick out one box of cereal to be your cereal for the week." I always sat there stunned by all the choices before me. There were Rice Krispies and Fruity Pebbles. There were Cocoa Puffs and Lucky Charms. There was Cookie Crisp, which was my personal favorite, and so many more. I ran up and down the aisle looking at the choices, trying to decide which one would be my cereal for the week.

Now on one particular trip, I was getting ready to choose my favorite Cookie Crisp (after all, who can resist chocolate chip cookies for breakfast?). But then, all of a sudden, a cereal I had never seen before caught my eye. It was called something like Fiber Bran[1]. Now nobody really eats Fiber Bran. It's one of those cereals for old people with issues that we don't like to talk about. But the reason this box of cereal caught my eye was that on the corner of the box, it had an advertisement that said something like "Free Spider-Man figure inside." I loved Spider-Man. Suddenly this trip to the grocery store felt like Christmas morning. Could there really be a Spider-Man figure in this box of Fiber Bran? My 6-year-old mind started getting the best of me. I turned the box over to investigate. On the back of the cereal box, the Spider-Man figure looked HUGE! My mind went to work again. If the Spider-Man figure was that big, there couldn't be much Fiber Bran in the box. I wanted the Spider-Man figure so badly, and I knew there was no way my mom was going to buy me such a toy on this trip. But now I had an opportunity to get it. Within this box of cereal was a way to get what I had been dreaming about — and mom wouldn't even realize what my grand plan was!

---

[1] I'm not sure what the actual name of the cereal was. In truth, this story is probably the compilation of many grocery store moments that run together as one in my childhood memory. But Fiber Bran is sufficiently bland to serve the purpose of the illustration.

I was faced with a choice: Fiber Bran or Cookie Crisp? Each option tugged at my soul. But the draw of the promised Spider-Man figure was a little larger. Before I knew it, I was running back to my mom with the box of Fiber Bran, asking her to put it in the grocery cart. You can imagine her stunned expression and surprised tone when she looked at me and said, "Fiber Bran?" To which I quickly answered, "Yeah, it's my new favorite!" She put the cereal in the cart. I had done it! The Spider-Man figure was about to be mine.

It seemed to take forever for us to make our way through the checkout line and head home. All I could think about was that Spider-Man figure and the hours of play and joy he would bring to my life. In fact, I wanted it so badly that I asked to eat Fiber Bran for dinner. But mom already had her plan for dinner that night. After I went to bed, I tossed and turned, anxiously awaiting the morning sunrise so that I could make my way to the kitchen and claim my prize. At six o'clock in the morning, I sprung out of my bed (I even made it that morning) and bolted down the stairs. I got out the stool to reach into the pantry for the box of Fiber Bran that had been placed a little out of my reach. Finally, the moment I had been anticipating was here. I jammed my hands down inside the cereal box like little kids often do. I searched around. And then, at last, I found the prize I had longed for. I pulled it out of the box, and…

Well let's just say I've been disappointed before in my life, but this was an entirely new level of disappointment. When I pulled that toy out of the box, it was about two inches big. And it was one of those cheap plastic figures that you can only play with twice before it breaks. My expectations were crushed. Even worse, now I sat there staring at an entire box of Fiber Bran. It was disgusting. In fact, I'm pretty sure it might still be in my mom's pantry today — and she has moved two times since then.

I had traded substance of cereal for a toy, and the tradeoff that promised so much on the front end couldn't live up to its lure.

I begin our journey together with that story because I think it points to a basic truth about us that is primary to our understanding of the revolution into which

I am inviting us. This is a tendency that in some ways I recognized from the earliest moments I started teaching and preaching. Over the years, I've become convinced it is increasingly true about us and the way we understand life spiritually. You and I are easily swayed by toys. On the back of the world's boxes, the toys look huge. And while Spider-Man figures may no longer tempt us, if you and I aren't careful, we will find ourselves trading the substance of our faith for something that promises more but in the end fails to deliver.

Unfortunately, it's not just the world that has bought into this tendency. Christianity too has bought in. We've shined up our toys and tweaked our gospel and theology just a bit in an effort to make it a compelling sell to the world around us. We've over-emphasized some things and intentionally left out others. We've promised people the world, and in the end we've left the world with just another cheap toy. We've gained a religion but lost our faith.

We've become toy soldiers, battling to get a cheap prize and missing out on the substance of our faith.

The Danish philosopher and Christian writer Soren Kierkegaard said it this way: "There are, in the end, only two ways open to us — to honestly and honorably make an admission of how far we are from the Christianity of the New Testament, or to perform skillful tricks to conceal the true situation." Unfortunately, we have become great at performing skillful tricks and concealing the true situation.

The result is that our main missional task has been distorted. Because we have chosen to make converts to a nice and neatly organized religion instead of making disciples of a radical and revolutionary faith, we have turned the gospel into something very different than the gospel writers intended it to be. Because we have pushed for a decision instead of a life of continual decisions, because we have held out the carrot of heaven as the reward for anyone who will sign a card or make the right statement of belief, we have built churches where people say they believe in Christ but never really follow him. Discipleship and mission have become secondary add-ons for those who have time to fill rather than primary components of which life with Christ is made.

In this quest to convert the world, most importantly we've forgotten that conversion was never Jesus' intention. We've forgotten that our call always was and always is to make disciples. And we've forgotten that, to make disciples, you actually have to be one. So it shouldn't surprise us when we find ourselves standing at the bottom of the pantry or sitting around the kitchen table asking why our lives and the lives around us look very little like Jesus. In this moment it slowly begins to dawn on us that we have only been converts ourselves. This is not enough — and we know it.

Converts are not disciples. And unfortunately they rarely become disciples. But they have replaced disciples in today's religion of Christianity. Converts believe stuff because they want to get to a place. Who we are as people is incidental at worst or a means to an end at best. What converts are really after is the toy.

Disciples are different. Disciples are following a person. That person is leading them toward a destination of sorts, but the journey is about more than moving from one place to another. Where they are going and who they are following actually start to change who they are becoming. The destination actually starts happening along the way.

The good news is that the way things are doesn't have to be the way things stay. In fact, you probably wouldn't be reading this book if that were true. Thankfully, normal can be redefined. And this can happen in and through ordinary people like you and me. Discipleship can once again replace conversion as the standard operating procedure of Christianity. And if it does it will keep us from settling for too little substance and too many cheap toys.

Many of you know this from firsthand experience. You too have begun the journey toward becoming Christ's disciple. Others of you may only be contemplating the journey.

Either way, this call in some ways may feel like learning a foreign language. You might like the way it sounds and might really like to speak it, but in the end you are just not sure that you have the time or capacity to do so. And because so many other people are speaking the common language of conversion, it's easy to reason that the masses must have it right. Even if you believe that discipleship instead of conversion is the right language, you may wonder if it's worth all the trouble of learning it.

But in this moment, I would like to appeal to the still small voice inside of you. I would like to appeal to the place in your heart, soul, and gut where you often recognize truth before you understand it. I appeal to that part of you because I think you already know the answer there. And I believe that deep inside, you want to see things change. I think you want to be called to be a disciple. I think you want to be encouraged to pursue that calling. And I think most of all that you might be seeking to find out what it all means and if it can deliver.

CHAPTER
TWO

Mirror Mayhem

"As a disciple of Jesus... I am learning from Jesus to live my life as he would live my life if he were I. I am not necessarily learning to do everything he did, but I am learning how to do everything I do in the manner that he did all that he did." — Dallas Willard

"After this, Jesus went out
and saw a tax collector
by the name of Levi sitting
at his tax booth. 'Follow me,'
Jesus said to him, and Levi got up,
left everything and followed him."
—Luke 5:27-28

*T*alking about discipleship is difficult. In fact, it's downright scary. It's scary not just because of what it might call us to become but also because we rarely really understand what IT is. In other words, many of us who talk about IT do so in ways that really aren't IT, or are at best only partially IT. The reason we know this is the case is because if IT were IT, then more people would probably be IT.

So the last thing I want to do is produce one more resource that misses the mark. And yet, I feel compelled to at least try to talk about IT, even if this discussion is also incomplete.

Discipleship is a word that everyone uses, and yet no one really knows what it means. It's not that the word means nothing to people. Instead, this word means a million different things to people. And because it means a million different things, it actually means nothing. Therefore, in the end many of us feel like we are chasing after the wind (or least chasing after the newest Christian fad or resource) when it comes to being Jesus' disciple. Of course, it's not that such resources are necessarily bad. We just don't have any grid through which to see them. So as we try to keep up with the newest ideas or causes, we become lots of different Christian kinds of things, and we hope that it somehow makes us a disciple. What we need is a framework to help it all make sense.

But Dallas Willard, in his book *The Divine Conspiracy*, describes his life of discipleship this way: "As a disciple of Jesus… I am learning from Jesus to live my life as he would live my life if he were I. I am not necessarily learning to do everything he did, but I am learning how to do everything I do in the manner that he did all that he did."[2] In other words, for Willard discipleship is not about becoming who Jesus was. It is about becoming who Jesus would be if Jesus were him.

---

[2] Dallas Willard, *The Divine Conspiracy* (San Francisco, HarperSanFrancisco, 1998) 283.)

I have heard lots of different definitions and articulations of discipleship, but I don't think I have ever heard a better description of discipleship than this. Discipleship is learning to become who Jesus would be if he were you. It starts with Jesus. Jesus is the one we get our cues from. But discipleship ends with us.

We look to Jesus to discover and experience what life is all about. But we don't merely try to become Jesus. Rather we invite Jesus to live his life in us. In this way, we not only begin to look like Jesus, but we also begin to look like the truest version of ourselves.

Who Do You Look Like?

Every once in a while, people will come up to me and tell me that I look like someone else. Sometimes this is a compliment. At other times, I wish they would have kept their opinion to themselves. My friends look like other people too. I have one friend who looks a lot like Richard Gere. I have another friend who resembles Tim Robbins. One other friend thinks he looks like Bruce Willis, but to everyone else he looks like Sam from the *Lord of the Rings* movies.

No matter whom others say we look like, one thing is unavoidably true: In the end we all wind up looking like our parents. We can try to avoid it all we want. We can spike our hair and tattoo our bodies to carve out our own identities. But none of that can shield us from the statement that people make straight to our face: "You look just like your dad — or your mom."

Looking like your mom or dad can be a good thing or a bad thing. If your mom and dad are attractive, you'd probably be OK hearing that you looked like them. But if your mom and dad look a little odd, you might cringe a little at this idea.

Now when someone says you look like your mom or your dad, you know a couple of things. First, you know that you don't look exactly like them. There are some characteristics about you that are unique to you. Second, you know that you carry their resemblance. People see it in your laugh or in your smile or in the way you mope. They see it in your eyes and sometimes around your stomach. But make no mistake, they see it. And if you look close enough and honestly enough, so will you.

So who do you look like? Not just in your outer appearance but in your inner soul. Who do you resemble? And does thinking about this question make you happy, or does it make you cringe a little?

Being a disciple of Jesus means living a life that resembles his life. People should be able to see him in our eyes, so to speak. And even though there are certain things that will always be unique to us, if we look in the mirror long enough we should begin to see him too.

Follow Me

The process of looking like or becoming like Jesus starts with two words. They are words that Jesus gave his earliest disciples. They are words that Jesus gave Peter twice, once at the beginning of his ministry and the other after Peter convinced himself he no longer belonged to group.[3] They are the words "Follow me." With these two words, Jesus invited an unlikely crew of motley men to take on his life. He invited them to embody his characteristics and his way. He invited them to be his family and carry on his resemblance in their DNA. And many of them did end up looking a lot like him, even if it took them a while to do so.

The problem today, though, is that it seems like everyone is saying "follow me" to us. People want us to sign up to follow them on Twitter. From the time we are little, we play follow the leader in which one person stands in front of us and calls us to mimic his or her behavior. But most of all, Jesus speaks these two words to us today, just as he spoke them to the disciples. These words call us to leave our other allegiances. These words call us to go where Jesus goes and value what he values. And these words call us to do all this as only we can.

You were not called to be me. I was not called to be you. But we were both called to follow Jesus. As we follow him, we will start to resemble him. And as we resemble

---

[3] See Luke 5 and John 21, as well as Mark 16, where Jesus told Mary to tell the disciples and Peter that he is risen. Peter would not have seen much of Jesus in himself when he denied him, yet Jesus reaffirmed the journey of discipleship to Peter in John 21. As a result, Peter looks remarkably like Jesus by Acts 3.

him, some things about each of us will look remarkably the same, while other things will make us very distinct. That's because, in the end, we are masterpieces, not machines.

Masterpieces vs. Machine

In the Western world, when we think of something being made, we often think of the assembly line process popularized in the Industrial Revolution. Using an assembly line, manufacturers could ensure that every product looked and functioned the same way. This ensured a standard of excellence and maximum efficiency. Sadly, all too often we turn the discipleship process into this kind of assembly line. We want everyone to look the same. We standardize the process. It's efficient, but it's not the best way to become a disciple of Christ and the truest version of ourselves. That's because the process is meant for machines, not for people.

Maybe a better approach is to think of the discipleship process the way a painter sees her artwork. Of course, there will be similar themes that run throughout all her paintings. Most of her artwork will have a certain look or style to it. But each masterpiece will be uniquely different. It's not that there is not a process. There is a process. But this process is much less about *standardization* and more about *specification*.

Listen to Paul as he articulates this kind of approach to discipleship in his letter to the Ephesians:

> As for you, you were dead in your transgressions and sins, in which you used to live when you followed the ways of this world and of the ruler of the kingdom of the air, the spirit who is now at work in those who are disobedient. All of us also lived among them at one time, gratifying the cravings of our flesh and following its desires and thoughts. Like the rest, we were by nature deserving of wrath. But because of his great love for us, God, who is rich in mercy, made us alive with Christ even when we were dead in transgressions – it is by grace you have been saved. And God raised us up with Christ and seated us with him in the heavenly

realms in Christ Jesus, in order that in the coming ages he might show the incomparable riches of his grace, expressed in his kindness to us in Christ Jesus. For it is by grace you have been saved, through faith — and this is not from yourselves, it is the gift of God — not by works, so that no one can boast. For we are God's handiwork, created in Christ Jesus to do good works, which God prepared in advance for us to do. (Ephesians 2:1-10)

Resemblance

Sameness was not the aim of Jesus for his disciples, nor was it Paul's hope for the believers in Ephesus. Instead, Jesus' aim was resemblance. Uniformity was not Jesus' call for his followers in John 17. Rather, he prayed for unity and for his life in them. Unity assumes that we are different. Jesus' life in us shows us how we are somewhat similar. Putting the two together isn't something that happens on an assembly line; instead, it must be a work of art. For this to happen, Jesus had to invest in his disciples and relate to them in different ways, like the way an artist delivers a masterpiece (or as Paul puts it in Ephesians, his "handiwork"). This is not the way most of us in the Western world think of processes, but maybe it's the way we should think of the process of discipleship.

Discipleship is about living our lives in a way that picks up the family resemblance of Christ in us. It's about living our lives like Jesus would if he were us — if he worked where we work, lived where we lived, had our giftings, and struggled with our limitations. As we begin resembling Jesus in this way, we also become the truest version of ourselves. This will happen in some similar ways and in some different ways in each of us. But if we pursue this kind of discipleship long enough, we may look in the mirror one day and catch a glimpse of Jesus' face. Or even better, maybe one day someone might come to up to us and tell us, "You look just like your brother."

CHAPTER
THREE

Pilgrim's Progress

"As we mature in Christ a Copernican revolution takes place where we go from thinking about God as a part of our life to the realization that we are a part of his life." — Richard Foster

"I consider everything a loss
because of the surpassing worth
of knowing Christ Jesus my Lord,
for whose sake I have lost all things.
I consider them garbage, that
I may gain Christ and be found in him."
—Philippians 3:8-9

S ometimes in life our biggest mistakes come not from our initial missteps but from our tendency of overcorrection.

Growing up in central Florida in the late 1980s and early '90s, it was impossible not to be a Miami Hurricane football fan. Miami was a dynasty. They didn't just win — they humiliated their opponents. Expectations were large, and anything less than a national championship was considered a down year. And at the height of Miami's success were a series of field goal attempts that defined Miami's rivalry with its chief nemesis Florida State. Three times, Florida State had the opportunity to dethrone the 'Canes. Had they won these games, Florida State would have been the dynasty instead of Miami. Three times a Florida State kicker lined up to win the game with one swing of his leg. Twice the kicker missed right. The third time he missed left.

It's the third kick that I want to take a moment to pause and think about. Twice in Florida State football history, a Seminole field-goal kicker had lost the game by pushing the ball right. The space between goat and glory on both of these kicks was about one foot. As a result "Wide right" became a slogan that defined Florida State football and especially their rivalry with the almighty Hurricanes. So it's not hard to imagine the anxiety that Florida State kicker Xavier Beitia felt as he lined up to try to win the game on October 12, 2002. Memories, as well as chants of "Wide right" from Hurricane fans, filled the air. A helpless Bobby Bowden wondered on the sidelines if maybe this time his kicker would get it right. (pun intended)

As time was running out, the ball was snapped. The snap was good. The hold was good. The kick looked clean. Only this time instead of missing wide right, Beitia missed wide left.

I remember watching the game and celebrating Florida State's demise. But even in my celebration, part of my heart went out to Bobby Bowden and the Florida State football team and especially to Xavier Beitia. With all the pressure not to miss right, Xavier was almost pushed into missing left. A new chant — "Wide right, wide right, wide left!" — was born.

The tendency that Xavier Beitia fell prey to in 2002 is the same tendency that many of us fall prey to every day. We see something wrong. And instead of correcting the problem, we over-correct. In the end, we wind up in a worse situation than our first initial mistake put us in.

Think about car accidents. Many wrecks happen when someone runs off one side of the road and, in an instant attempt to get back on the road, the driver overcorrects and swerves into oncoming traffic or off the road into the trees on the other side.

The problem of overcorrection also happens to apply to God-following.

We see a mistake of a certain set of God followers, but instead of correcting the mistake we overcorrect it. So instead of running into one ditch, we head into another. This is especially true in our relationship with the process of discipleship.

The Process of Specification

When it comes to discipleship and following God, there are basically two types of people. One group has a plan and strategy and process for everything. These people want everyone to follow their plan and strategy and process so that in the end everyone will look the same. This usually produces an equal and opposite reaction from people who refuse to follow any plan or strategy or process at all. In their striving to be unique, this second group overcorrects and resists the wrong thing.

Thankfully, there is a different way. It begins by resisting standardization instead of resisting process. It understands that process itself is not the enemy. In fact, many times significant progress comes through a process. This different way teaches us to lean into process if it's the right kind of process. And what is the right kind of process? One that produces *specification* instead of *standardization*.

26

To help us along the way and begin this process of specification, I want to introduce you to an equation that may help cement what I am talking about in your mind. But before I introduce it, I want to state clearly that this is an equation and not a formula. Equations help us find and evaluate truth. Formulas tell us exactly what to do and in what order to do it.

Many people have given formulas for Christian growth. This is not another one. Rather, this is an equation that I hope will help us better articulate what we are going for when it comes to following Jesus and how we can recognize moments when we do resemble him.

The Equation of Resemblance
The equation is derived from simple algebra. Now I know some you are thinking that simple algebra is an oxymoron. And I get that. But hang with me — I promise we won't get too complex.

We are all familiar with a standard variable equation that looks something like this:

$$\frac{5}{10} = \frac{X}{30}$$

We can solve for X in this equation in several different ways. Some of us could solve the equation on pure recognition — for some almost unknown reason we just know the answer intuitively. Others of us might solve it through cross multiplication and division. Still others might work from trial and error. But in the end, the answer that we all hope to get to is 15. The first fraction serves to set the standard. The second fraction helps us establish an equivalent pattern and congruent answer. But there is one, best answer. Fourteen would be too little. Sixteen would be too much.

Now let's take the discipleship process and build from the truth that we all recognize in this mathematical equation. Here is the equation that I suggest might help us understand what the life of the disciple looks like:

$$\frac{\text{The life Jesus lived}}{\text{Who Jesus was}} = \frac{\text{X (The life I should live)}}{\text{Who I am}}$$

This equation can also be solved in different ways. But regardless of how we solve it, we can use this equation begin to measure how congruent to Christ our lives are. Some things will be necessary for all of our journeys. A healthy understanding of numeric value, multiplication, and division and their spiritual corollaries will help everyone.

But because the denominators on our side of the equation will be different for each of us, our numerators will have to be different as well. We will both be patterned after Jesus, but because the denominator of who we are is intrinsically different, the display of Christ in our lives will necessarily be unique. This process of specification allows us to all study Christ (and we could expand the equation to God in general), but it also allows for our expressions of him to be tailored to fit our personalities, strengths, weaknesses, and giftings.

Copernican Revolutions

It is important to remember that this kind of evaluation is not arbitrary. We can't make X anything we want. We can't simply invite Jesus to be part of our life. Instead, all of our life is derived from his life. We are letting his life inform, evaluate, and project the trajectory our lives take. If we do this, we will experience more than Jesus getting in on part of our life. Instead, what we will find is that we are actually getting in on his life.

I love the way that Richard Foster describes this in his book *Prayer: Finding the Heart's True Home* (which is less a book on prayer and more a book on spiritual formation): "As we mature in Christ a Copernican Revolution takes place where we go from thinking about God as a part of our life to the realization that we are a part of his life."[4] Copernicus challenged the system of his day by suggesting

---

[4] Richard J. Foster, *Prayer* (San Francisco, HarperSanFrancisco, 1992) 15.

that the sun didn't revolve around the earth but instead that the earth revolved around the sun. That challenge resulted in him being branded a heretic. But it eventually changed the way science and all of us see the entire universe.

The same can happen in our lives. We can no longer settle for Jesus being part of our lives. Rather, discipleship calls us to draw all of our life from his life. This will be a task of theology, and it will be a task of psychology and sociology as well. We will have to study God, and we will have to discover our selves. We will need to know Jesus intimately and know our true selves as well.

I overhear this kind of Copernican revolution in Paul's burst of passion in his letter to the Philippians:

> But whatever were gains to me I now consider loss for the sake of Christ. What is more, I consider everything a loss because of the surpassing worth of knowing Christ Jesus my Lord, for whose sake I have lost all things. I consider them garbage, that I may gain Christ and be found in him, not having a righteousness of my own that comes from the law, but that which is through faith in Christ — the righteousness that comes from God on the basis of faith. I want to know Christ — yes, to know the power of his resurrection and participation in his sufferings, becoming like him in his death, and so, somehow, attaining to the resurrection from the dead. Not that I have already obtained all this, or have already arrived at my goal, but I press on to take hold of that for which Christ Jesus took hold of me. Brothers and sisters, I do not consider myself yet to have taken hold of it. But one thing I do: Forgetting what is behind and straining toward what is ahead, I press on toward the goal to win the prize for which God has called me heavenward in Christ Jesus. (Philippians 3:7-14)

The interesting thing about Paul is that he didn't only want to know and identify with Christ; he actually *did* it. Luke makes this clear to us in the Acts of the Apostles, where we see a striking similarity in how the life of Paul is described and the life that Jesus lived. Luke makes no apology in setting Paul up as the "Jesus" of Acts.[5]

Paul actually did the same thing in his writings. Paul told the Corinthian church to "imitate him as he imitates Christ." (1 Corinthians 11:1) In other words, Paul told these disciples that if they modeled their lives after him, they would begin to resemble Christ to some extent. How could he say this? Because it was true. His life did resemble Christ's life. He had developed the X Factor.

So we see the Equation of Resemblance embodied in Paul and passed on to the Corinthian believers. Paul sent Timothy to them as another person in the pattern. The X Factor was in all of them, and it is being passed to us as well. The question is whether or not we will submit to the process.

What Do You Want?

As I was finishing writing this chapter, I saw it again. The only difference was that this time it wasn't Florida State; it was Boise State. With a potential invitation to the national championship game on the line, Kyle Brotzman missed a potential game-winning field goal to the right in the final seconds. In overtime he missed a go-ahead field goal left. He had overcorrected.

Left to our own devices we will do the same. We will miss in one direction and overcorrect in the other. We need a process that we can evaluate our lives by, one that will call us into something better. What we find in Paul helps us do this, I think. But we have to want it.

We have to want to know Christ — not just an intellectual understanding of him, but an understanding that includes our *head*, our *heart* and our *hands*. And by knowing him, we also have to want to identify with him. We have to want our way of life to be born out of his way of life. We must want our side of the

---

[5] Idea taken from an Introduction to New Testament lecture by my mentor Danny Goodman.

equation to be congruent with his side of the equation. And even more, we need to want to see what change results in the world when we decide to orient our lives around his.

While it may not be possible for us to actually be Jesus, it is possible for me to become who Jesus would be if he were me. It is possible for you to become who Jesus would be if he were you as well. So let's get started solving the equation together. And let's try to kick it through the uprights this time.

CHAPTER
FOUR

A Matter of Life and Death

"The Christian ideal has not been tried and found wanting,
rather it has been found difficult and left untried."
— G.K. Chesterton

"Whoever wants to be my disciple
must deny themselves and
take up their cross daily
and follow me."
—Luke 9:23-24

*I*T'S NOT WORTH IT! When is the last time you said these words or had them on the tip of your tongue? For some of us, it may have been the last time we got paid our allowance. When I was a little kid, I did my list of chores for the reward of only a couple dollars a week. In chapter one, I talked about how raking leaves never made sense to me. The fact that my parents only paid two dollars to rake the whole yard made the chore even worse. Basically, my dad was not aware of the child labor laws in our state. And that couple of dollars was before inspection. With 30 cents taken off here, and a dollar deducted there, before you know it I was paying my parents to do my chores. That's when the four words "It's not worth it" came to the front of my mind. (Now, 20 years later now, the same thing happens with the allowance my wife gives me.)

For others of us, these words rose up in us the last time we put a puzzle together. I like puzzles, but I'm a 20-piece puzzle guy. Everyone once in a while, though, I get pulled into putting a 500-piece or 1,000-piece puzzle together. Three hours into the process, when I've found only two pieces that fit together, these four words "It's not worth it" come racing to my mind.

Maybe these words come to mind when you watch your favorite football team. I live in South Carolina, and I can tell you that these words far too often resonate with fans of Clemson University, one of the local teams. If you happen to be a Clemson football fan, these words tend to describe every Saturday in the fall as you sit down really believing that maybe this week will be the week you win a big game and rise to national prominence. Unfortunately, by halftime these four words "It's not worth it" are once again right on the tip of your tongue as you realize that your team has underachieved. Whether you're a Clemson fan, or a fan of another underachieving team, you know this feeling all too well.

For me, these four words come to mind every time I go running. I grew up playing soccer, and I played soccer in college. But I have never liked running. I don't mind running after a ball. However, running just to run leads to a constant negotiation in my mind. After the first five minutes, I'm looking for holes that I could step in and potentially break my ankle so that I won't have to feel guilty about stopping — or about avoiding running for the next eight weeks or so. Some people speak of a runner's high that come right after you break through the runner's wall. This has not been my experience. Behind every runner's wall that I break through, I only find more runner's walls. My only fleeting experience with any sort of runner's high came in the Mexican restaurant after the race was over. And so when I run, these four words "It's not worth it" are constantly on my mind.

Now let's ask a bigger question. When was the last time these four words "It's not worth it" were on the tip of your tongue when it comes to God? If it is has been a while, then I want to make a kind of odd suggestion to you. Maybe you are not taking God seriously enough. The reason I say that is because these four words "It's not worth it" are the words that come to our minds whenever life gets hard. And sometimes following God is hard. His way is always best, but it is rarely easy. Sometimes life makes it look like God can't be trusted. Sometimes God calls us to give up that which feels natural to us and encourages us to take the road less traveled. And it's often in these moments that these four words "It's not worth it" stand on the tip of our tongues with God.

The tough part about all this, though, is that it is precisely in these moments, when these four words are on the tip of our tongue, that we should have the most confidence that we are actually on the right trail. Think about it this way: Often the road to death at first feels like life. And often the road to life at first appears a lot like death. That is because the road of life is a death of sorts. It's a letting go, so to speak. It's a continual surrender.

Life and Death in Jesus

We can't talk about following Jesus without talking about the cross. Jesus himself told us that this cross will come. Listen to him in Luke 9:23-24: "Then he said to them all: 'Whoever wants to be my disciple must deny themselves and take up their cross daily and follow me. For whoever wants to save their life will lose it, but whoever loses their life for me will save it.'"

So becoming a disciple means dying to certain things. However, it's important to understand that we die not just because Jesus is in love with death, but because through death resurrection is possible. The same Jesus who told us to take up our cross and follow him also made this declaration about himself in John 10:10: "I have come so that they might have life and have it to the max.[6]" His goal is not death, but rather the kind of life that comes through resurrection.

To live the life that Jesus would live if he were us, we will have to die to the life we would live without him. And we also have to pursue resurrection. We don't die well by pursuing death. But when we pursue resurrection, we end up dying well.

Learning to die well and to pursue a resurrected kind of life is how we solve the Equation of Resemblance.

This kind of life doesn't always come easy to us. That's why, just as we need the basic math of numeric value, multiplication, and division to help us solve an algebraic equation, we need to learn the basic pathway of Christian discipleship to help us pursue resurrection and die well.

The Pathway

The basic math or basic pathway of solving X in the Equation of Resemblance is that of *information*, *imitation* and *imagination*. I picture these ideas in a circle with arrows moving in each direction.

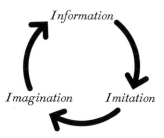

---

[6] "To the max" is my paraphrase of what Scripture says. I use it because it captures Jesus' meaning as well as any phrase could.

While these three things are necessary to us dying to our old way of life and living the resurrected kind of life that Jesus would live if he were us, they don't necessarily happen all the time or in any certain order. The order is interchangeable, but the presence of each of the three is necessary. Let's talk about all three and the way they function to form the discipleship pathway that helps us solve for X in the Equation of Resemblance in our lives.

Information

Information is the basic knowledge of the person and the way of God that we encounter through the revelation of Bible, in the gospel, by building a theology, and via spiritual disciplines. Each of these pathways helps us discover interesting facts about God but even more discover God himself. And in the end, the best representation of God is found in Jesus. By understanding the personhood of God as found in the person and work of Jesus, we can begin to work on the left side of the equation. Remember, it is the life Jesus lived and the person Jesus is that forms the standard for the discipleship process. Therefore, constantly discovering and continually committing to increasing our revelation of him is the primary way to become his disciple. Revolution comes through revelation. We will explore the idea of information more fully in the next section of the book.

Imitation

Imitation is the way we see Jesus' life lived out in others. It is also the way we pass on the way of Christ to those who come behind us. Learning from those who have gone before us on this journey is important. Seeing the Christ pattern in their actual lives helps us begin to see what our lives could actually look like when we form them based on this pattern. In this way, the life of Christ comes to us here and now, not just there and then. As we watch others, the world of Bible transforms into the world of today. And so when we use our lives to demonstrate the life of Christ to those who come behind us, we too join the long list of the faithful who ensure that the life of faith and Christ-following continues into the world of tomorrow. This part of the discipleship process expands through mentors, friends and colleagues, and mentees. We'll develop these ideas more fully in section three of this book.

Imagination

Imagination is the way that we actually live out Christ's life through our lives. It's how we eventually work to solve for X in the right side of the equation. As we discover Christ in revelation and take our baby steps toward his life in imitation, imagination helps us discover how we can fully realize his life in ours. It takes into account our personality, strengths, weaknesses, giftings, and limitations. It helps us rethink who we are and what our lives should become. Even more, it helps us bring about systems in which his life can be best manifested in others. It's what helps Christ's life change us and then change everything through his work in us. Section four of this book will deal with these ideas.

The Christian Ideal

In all of these things, we work toward what some might consider to be the Christian ideal — a life congruent to Christ's life. This is the road less traveled, but it is the road that you and I were created to walk down. The great Christian writer and thinker G.K. Chesterton once wrote, "The Christian ideal has not been tried and found wanting, rather it has been found difficult and left untried." Our job is to make sure that this quote of Chesterton does not become the history of God-following in our generation. So we must spend our lives pursuing the continual collision of our life and God's life through the pathway of information, imitation, and imagination.

This path will mean death, but it will also bring life. And though this road of discipleship will rarely be easy, remember these four words: IT IS WORTH IT!

SECTION
TWO

The 411

We have pushed hard in our understanding of discipleship so far to move from discipleship being simply a statement of belief toward understanding discipleship as a life of faith. This is a critical adjustment for us to make. But it would be a mistake for us to think that discipleship is separate from an understanding of reality. In other words, following Christ is a way of life, but following Christ is also more than a way of life. Jesus is more than a role model. Being a Christian requires more than believing that Jesus lived well.

As much as Christian discipleship is a movement of Spirit, it is also a movement of truth. It's a way of life based on a set of assertions – assertions about God and about Jesus and about life.

Now we are going to shift our conversation to talk about how we think about and engage the truth of God in our lives.

This engagement of truth though is not in opposition to Spirit. In fact, the two were never meant to be separated. Each gives way to the other, in the same way that each member of the Trinity gives way to one another. So this search for truth is also a movement of Spirit, and if it's done well, it will help us Redefine Normal and begin to solve for X in the Equation of Resemblance.

All this brings up another important point: Can we handle the truth? Of all discussions about truth I've ever heard, one stands above the rest in my memory. It's the discussion Tom Cruise and Jack Nicholson have in the captivating concluding scene of *A Few Good Men*. As Nicholson (Colonel Nathan Jessep) sits on the witness stand, Cruise (Lieutenant Daniel Kaffee) relentlessly examines him. Finally in a heated moment, Cruise demands the truth, which leads to the following exchange:

> Col. Jessep: You want answers?
> Lt. Kaffee: I think I'm entitled.
> Col. Jessep: (shouting) You want answers?
> Lt. Kaffee: (shouting) I want the truth!
> Col. Jessep: (shouting) You can't handle the truth! (deliberately) Son, we

live in a world that has walls, and those walls have to be guarded by men with guns. Who's gonna do it? You? You, Lt. Weinburg? I have a greater responsibility than you could possibly fathom. You weep for Santiago, and you curse the Marines. You have that luxury. You have the luxury of not knowing what I know. That Santiago's death, while tragic, probably saved lives. And my existence, while grotesque and incomprehensible to you, saves lives. You don't want the truth because deep down in places you don't talk about at parties, you want me on that wall, you need me on that wall. We use words like honor, code, loyalty. We use these words as the backbone of a life spent defending something. You use them as a punchline. I have neither the time nor the inclination to explain myself to a man who rises and sleeps under the blanket of the very freedom that I provide, and then questions the manner in which I provide it. I would rather you just said thank you, and went on your way, Otherwise, I suggest you pick up a weapon, and stand a post. Either way, I don't (care) what you think you are entitled to.

For us as well, the question behind our discussion on truth and revelation is whether we can handle the truth.

Now, that's not the question that most people associate with revelation. Most people wonder if we will find truth, not if we can handle it. But at the heart of the Bible and especially of the ministry of Jesus, the question of finding truth is not the most important question. In my experience, most people don't give up on following God because they can't find truth. They give up on following God because they don't know how to handle the truth that they find.

Finding God many times calls us to change, and lots of times we don't want to change. So instead of leaning into the truth that may cause us to change, we settle for believing something less than truth so that we can stay the same. But this is not the way it should be. Handling the truth and being willing to change based on what we find out about God is the key to Redefining Normal. Revelation must give birth to revolution. And this happens first in us before it happens through us.

That is, if we can handle it.

CHAPTER
FIVE

Picture Pages

"Earth's crammed with heaven, and every common bush
afire with God; but only he who sees takes off his shoes —
the rest just sit around and pluck blackberries."
— Elizabeth Barrett Browning

*"In the past God spoke to
our ancestors through the prophets
at many times and in various ways,
but in these last days he has spoken to us by
his Son, whom he appointed heir of all things,
and through whom also he made the universe.
The Son is the radiance of God's glory and the
exact representation of his being, sustaining all
things by his powerful word."
—Hebrews 1:1-3*

*I*f becoming a disciple requires us handling the truth, then we as Christians believe that there is no better source that helps us handle that truth than the Bible. Christians are people of the book so to speak — or at least we are supposed to be. We are people of the book because Jesus was a person of the book. We are people of the book because it is in the book that we find God's story and Jesus' life. For us, truth and knowledge of God are not something that we engage on our own. It is the quest of our community – and not just the community we interact with in the present, but the community of the ages. The community of the ages, alongside the active Spirit of God, has written the revelation of God that we know as the Bible. So the Bible is for us a primary source of information.

But just because we have the Bible doesn't mean we understand it. And just because we own a book that we refer to as a book of revelation doesn't mean that we have actually seen God revealed. And maybe that is because those of us who have a Bible too often forget that the Bible's primary work is that of showing us who God is. We forget that the Bible is the story of God in the past told to illuminate Him in the present. We forget that the same Spirit who helped those before us write it now also stands ready to help us understand it so that we see God in our midst. As a result we read the Bible without really seeing Him and hear it without really perceiving Him. And in the end, this blindness usually leads us to stop reading it and quit hearing it and start wondering what our life really has to do with it. And then we wonder where God is, even though He may be standing right in front of us.

Pink Elephants and 800-pound Gorillas

When was the last time you were with someone who just didn't get it? You know the person I'm talking about — someone who is oblivious to something that seems obvious to you, someone who is confused by what is clear to everyone else, someone who just can't see the Pink Elephant or the 800-pound gorilla standing right in front of him.

Redefining Normal

Maybe there's a better question: When was the last time that person was you?

In 2007, the *Washington Post* conducted a social experiment where a reporter asked world-class violinist Joshua Bell to spend a morning rush hour playing at a Washington, D.C. metro station. The reporter wanted to find out two things as he watched to see if anyone noticed the beautiful art on display:

1. Would the beauty of Joshua's music transcend a mundane setting and an inconvenient time?
2. How would people react to beautiful art when that art it is found in an unexpected environment?

Joshua, who was dressed in street clothes and had an open violin case beside him, played six classical pieces over 43 minutes. During that 43 minutes, the reporter counted 1,097 people who walked by. Of those 1,097 people, only 27 of them gave him money, totaling $32 and some change. Only seven stopped what they were doing to hang around and take in part of the performance. Sadly, the vast majority of people were so wrapped up in their own cares, worries, and business that they missed what was right in front of them. Some were listening to music on their iPods and never even heard the beautiful music. Still others heard but were just ignorant about what they were hearing.

Whatever the reason, it's amazing to think about just how many people missed the beauty that was in their presence that day. On a regular basis, Joshua Bell plays at night to sold-out concert halls filled with people who pay hundreds of dollars to hear him play and stand to applaud when he is done. But that morning in the D.C. metro station, this same man, performing the same songs he performs each night, had only seven people pause even for a minute. He received just 32 bucks as he stood and played his violin for anyone who would listen. And when he was done he got not even a single clap.

The reporter in this article came to a fascinating conclusion. Based on this experiment, he determined that there is no recognition factor whatsoever for beauty in people's lives. In other words, the reporter suggested that most people have to be told that something is beautiful before they see its beauty. We simply have trouble recognizing beauty on our own. And too often, we find ourselves oblivious to what should be obvious.[7]

I believe the same struggle to see beauty that we saw in the Washington D.C. metro station is also apparent in our struggle to see and hear God. The problem is not that God is not present in life. The problem is that often most of us don't notice Him. We need someone or something to tell us that God is present and to give us a picture of what he might look like in this situation.

Thankfully, we are not the first to have this struggle. The pages of the Bible are littered with people who at first missed God, only to find later that He had been all around them. For Samuel it happened in a late-night encounter when God called his name. Samuel, instead of recognizing God, ran to Eli three times. Finally Eli was the one who pointed Samuel to God.

Jacob wrestled with God one night across the ford of Jabbok. At first he thought he was wrestling with a man — maybe Laban, maybe Esau. Only later as Jacob walked by the setting of the wrestling match, which left him limping, did Jacob call it Peniel, which means "Face of God." For he saw God face to face, and yet his life was spared.

The guys on the road to Emmaus walked with Jesus one afternoon following his resurrection. But they didn't know they were walking with Jesus. Only when Jesus broke bread in their presence did they recognize him.

We too need someone or something to help us recognize God in our midst. That is what the Bible is all about. When we read it, study it, and meditate on it, it helps us see God. It helps us recognize Jesus.

---

[7] Gene Weingarten, "Pearls before breakfast," washingtonpost.com, 4-8-2007. I first used this illustration in The Domino Effect participants guide that the Wayfarer team wrote a few years back.

Photo Album

Because this is what the Bible does in our lives, one of the most helpful ways we can understand the Bible is to see it as a photo album, or as what those of you who are a little bit younger might know as an iPhoto slideshow. The Bible is a photo album or slideshow of God. It is a photo album or slideshow of life and death. In the Bible, the community of the ages gives us snapshots of God in the past. It gives us snapshots of what life with God looks like. Also, it gives us snapshots of what life apart from God looks like. By looking at this photo album, we can begin to recognize God and life as they stand in front of us every day. Here is how it might work:

Every summer I have the incredible opportunity to travel the country and speak to thousands of students at many different summer camps and conferences. It's one of the things I love about my job. But last summer, I had an experience that solidified the truth we're talking about once again in my life. I had gotten to one camp a little early so that I could take in my surroundings and prepare myself for students that were coming to Texas from Louisiana for this particular week of camp, and as I did I wandered almost accidentally into the worship room. The youth minister and the technicians were preparing the room for the services that were going to happen later that night. I meandered to the back of the room to listen as the band did its soundcheck.

That's when it happened. The youth minister came up to me, called me by my name and told me how glad he was to see me and how happy he was that I had arrived safely. The interesting thing about this is that I had never met this youth minister in person. Yet, with all the confidence in the world, he recognized me as I came in the room and bent over backward to acknowledge my presence. But how did he know it was me?

Although we had never actually met in person, he had seen me in pictures. We had talked on the phone. And maybe he had even seen a video clip of me speaking somewhere. Further, he was expecting to see me that day as I arrived for camp. So, when I came in he recognized me. He acknowledged me, and he did it with all the confidence in the world.

I'm convinced that this can be the Bible's greatest gift to us. It lets us see pictures of God in the past so that we can recognize Him in our lives in the present. As in every photo album, some pictures capture certain nuances or poses that do not convey the entirety of who we are. And as in every iPhoto slideshow, some pictures of us in our younger years show only glimmers of who we become as we grow older. So it is in the photo album or iPhoto slideshow of God. This is especially important as we try to understand and reconcile different pictures of God in the Old and New Testaments.

In the Bible, we encounter God through progressive revelation. So while the pictures of God in the Old Testament may be less complete, like baby pictures or awkward teenage snapshots are, we can always recognize God's presence best by looking in his eyes. (Now I'm not insinuating that God has grown up or changed. Instead, because the Bible is progressive revelation, our pictures of God grow up, so to speak, as the story progresses.) In Jesus we see God's most fully developed manifestation. But whether it is baby pictures, awkward teenage pictures, or more fully developed pictures like Jesus, all of these pictures help us see God today when he enters the room. And the truth is He is always in the room. We just need to expect him and to learn to recognize Him.

The written word helps us recognize the Living Word and take notice of His presence. Listen to Scripture as it points us to this truth in Hebrews: "In the past God spoke to our ancestors through the prophets at many times and in various ways, but in these last days he has spoken to us by his Son, whom he appointed heir of all things, and through whom also he made the universe. The Son is the radiance of God's glory and the exact representation of his being, sustaining all things by his powerful word." (Hebrews 1:1-3)

Redefining Normal
So here is the truth that may help us Redefine Normal when it comes to reading the Bible: *We don't read the Bible to please God. We read the Bible to see God.* God is not up in heaven keeping track of your devotional schedule. But God is waiting for you to see him. And he has given us the revelation of his Word to help us do so.

The same is true with life and death. By reading the pages of the Bible, we do not only see pictures of God. We also, through its characters and their choices, through proverbs and poetry and many other genres, get a glimpse of what life with God and life away from God might look like. The Bible helps us see the benefits of choosing to walk with God and the consequences of walking away from Him. And because history often repeats itself, it also helps us recognize these roads as they stand in front of us each day. So, if we will be students of the Bible, it will teach us to choose life.

So what if today you really began to believe that God was right in front of you? What if life and death were not as indistinguishable as you first thought? What if you had access to something that helped you recognize it all? Don't you think it might be worth your time to give it a look?

Well, the Bible is such a tool. It is waiting for you to discover it. It's not always easy to read and understand, and its pictures sometimes appear a bit hazy. But if you will read and listen in long enough, God and life might actually begin to come into focus, both in the past and in the present. And recognizing God in the present might just be the best present of all, because once you start seeing Him, you start seeing Him everywhere. But if you will hang around to hear Him play, you might just be fascinated by how beautiful the life He is inviting you into really is.

CHAPTER
SIX

Really Good News

"Preach the gospel to yourself every day."
— Martin Luther

*"Woe to me!" I cried.
"I am ruined! For I am a man
of unclean lips, and I live among
a people of unclean lips,
and my eyes have seen the King,
the LORD Almighty."
—Isaiah 6:5*

*S*eeing God can be good. It can also be… not so good. It's one thing for God to show up. It's another thing to try to relate to Him. Time after time in the Bible, as people begin to recognize the presence of God, they have the same response. They cower in fear and in awe. This is because when God shows up there is one truth that is overwhelmingly evident: we aren't him!

Listen to the words of Isaiah when God entered the temple and Isaiah got a glimpse of who God is: "In the year that King Uzziah died, I saw the Lord, high and exalted, seated on a throne; and the train of his robe filled the temple. Above him were seraphim, each with six wings: With two wings they covered their faces, with two they covered their feet, and with two they were flying. And they were calling to one another:

> "'Holy, holy, holy is the LORD Almighty; the whole earth is full of his glory.'
>
> "At the sound of their voices the doorposts and thresholds shook and the temple was filled with smoke. 'Woe to me!'" I cried. 'I am ruined! For I am a man of unclean lips, and I live among a people of unclean lips, and my eyes have seen the King, the LORD Almighty.'
>
> "Then one of the seraphim flew to me with a live coal in his hand, which he had taken with tongs from the altar. With it he touched my mouth and said, 'See, this has touched your lips; your guilt is taken away and your sin atoned for.'" (Isaiah 6:1-7)

Not only are we not God; we aren't anything like Him. In fact, the core definition of the word *holy*, which is the word used constantly to describe God, is not just *pure* but *other*. He is other than us. He is different than us. He is not like us.

But this is not the way it is supposed to be. We were created to be like God in a certain way. In fact, the opening chapters of the Bible tell us that God made us in his own image, something that was supposed to differentiate us from every other part of His creation. God created us "in his likeness." (Genesis 1:26) He wanted us to resemble him. He wanted us to represent him. He wanted us to live in love with Him.

Our problem is that we wanted to be like him in status but not in character. So just three chapters into the story of God and humankind, we walked away from God, crowned ourselves as god on our own behalf, and in the process not only defiled ourselves but the entire world. (Genesis 3 tells the story.) As a result, we lost the very essence of what we were created for. We became other than God, and so he became other than us. Where he was pure, we became marked by sin. Where he was healthy, we became sick. Where he was rich, we became poor. Where he was whole, we became empty. Where he was full of life, we became subject to death. We retained the image but we marred it in a certain way, so much so that when God showed up we felt not accepted but naked. We felt not love but fear. Today we still feel the ramifications of this ongoing decision that started with Adam and Eve and continues through us.

So how do we even begin to relate to this God? The answer to this question is *gospel*. Gospel is how God relates to humankind in our fallen state. It's how we get back to embracing how we were meant to be like Him. It's how we interact with Him. It's what makes life with Him possible.

Fortunately, despite our rebelliousness, God refuses to let our rebellion become the end of the story. In his grace and mercy, God chases after us. First, he chased us by fashioning a people for himself to live in covenant with him. Then as the fulfillment of this movement of people, he chased after us by working through his Son Jesus to complete that covenant on our behalf and invite us and the entire world into this ongoing kind of covenant relationship. The work of Jesus at the cross makes everything lost in The Fall recoverable again. Gospel is how God has done this.

Some of us have heard this story all our lives, and we might assume that we could move past this chapter without really reading it. But as is the case with the Bible, just because we have heard it doesn't mean we really understand it. In fact, personally I believe a skewed understanding of the gospel is what has made Redefining Normal so necessary. So let's take a minute to discover (or maybe rediscover) the gospel and how it leads us to redefine normal in our lives.

Toilet Paper

A couple of years ago, my wife Kim and I were getting ready to go out for a night on the town when she informed me that she had lost the $40 in cash that we were going to use for our night of festivities. Now, most of the time when someone in my marriage loses something, it's me. This time, however, my wife had lost it. Yet, still somehow it was my fault. (If you are married, you know how this works. It's always the guy's fault. Even if it's not the guy's fault, it is still his fault.) We looked and searched and scoured the house in search of the $40 that had been lost.

I did the typical guy thing while we searched. I tried to appear useful. My first 13 years of marriage have taught me that I don't have to actually *be* useful, but I must at least *appear to be* useful. I was looking in cabinets and cupboards. I was looking in dressers and drawers. I was looking in places that I hadn't looked since we bought the house five years earlier. I knew the $40 wasn't there, but I was looking anyway — just trying to appear useful.

Finally, after about 30 minutes of looking, my wife called out to me and said, "I found it! Or, at least part of it." That was a strange statement – one I hadn't heard her say before. I went to find her and to see what she had found. As I got back to our bedroom, I saw her in the master bathroom pulling a $20 bill out of the toilet. Now I have lost a lot of things in my time. But never once have I found what I was looking for in the toilet. We have no idea how the money got there. But there it was.

Amazingly, this is not the end of the story. Often in life, men and women see things very differently. And so my wife and I looked at this moment in time in very distinct ways. Kim was happy we got half of the $40 back. But I was thinking that since we found $20, why not go after the rest of it? So I headed to the other bathroom to get the plunger in a feat of manhood that seemed appropriate for such a time as this. All along the way, I got no encouragement from my life partner. It's not the way things used to be, but it is how things had evolved in 13 years of marriage. Back when we were dating, my wife found pretty much everything I said profound. Now when I say something like, "Let's get the plunger and plunge up the other $20," she just rolls her eyes and tells me it will never work. Still, because I'm a man and a little bit stubborn, I pursued what to me was the good idea of plunging the $20 out of the toilet. My wife was mocking me the whole time. (I hope you know that I say this all in good fun. Healthy sarcastic banter is what makes our relationship dynamic, and exciting and adventurous.)

I plunged the toilet hoping to retrieve the other $20 we had lost. I pushed the plunger down three times and pulled it back to see what would happen. And I'm happy to tell you that when I did, the other $20 came floating back up in the toilet. It was like a gift of God himself. It was as if God was looking down on me and validating me in my marriage by saying, "Well done, my good and faithful servant."

I tell you this story to bring up a few things. First, you never know where your money has been. Second, nothing is unrecoverable. No matter how bad things are, they can be restored. We don't have to stretch the metaphor too far to tell you that, even if your life feels like it is in the toilet, nothing is beyond the reach and grasp and grace of Jesus. And finally, I tell you this story to say that sometimes, when something valuable is lost, it's worth doing something crazy to recover it, even when you are being criticized to do so. As in the story that Jesus told in Luke 15 of a woman who cleaned her entire house to recover one coin, what is lost is sometimes actually most important.

Multifaceted Gospel

So what does all this have to do with the gospel? A lot, actually. I believe we live in a day when Biblical gospel understanding has been lost. Many traditions have recovered part of it, but few have kept pursuing all of it. As a result, we live in a day with multiple half-gospels masquerading as the whole thing. We have a sin gospel and a soul gospel. We have a prosperity gospel and a social gospel. We have a health gospel and a hell gospel. But in the end we have hardly any whole gospel at all. As a result too much is being left… well, in the toilet.

This brings up an interesting question. What then is the gospel? It is in this area that I think we may need to begin some of our most important work.

As we talk about the gospel, I think it is important that we distinguish between what Jesus referred to as wine and wineskin. In Jesus' analogy to describe the kingdom, he challenged the religious leaders of his day with these words: "No one sews a patch of unshrunk cloth on an old garment. Otherwise, the new piece will pull away from the old, making the tear worse. And no one pours new wine into old wineskins. Otherwise, the wine will burst the skins, and both the wine and the wineskins will be ruined. No, they pour new wine into new wineskins." (Mark 2:21-22)

What was true of the kingdom in Jesus' day is true of the gospel in our day, I believe. There are lots of wineskins that have been developed to hold part of the gospel. But the whole gospel ends up bursting the skin. So a distinguishing between wine and wineskin is vital if we are to recover a fuller gospel in our lives.

You see this pretty clearly when someone is asked to explain what they think the gospel is. Many times they start explaining what the gospel *means* more than what the gospel actually is. As they do so, they end up stating the gospel in ways that aren't actually in the gospels. This is not necessarily bad. It only becomes bad when we start to limit the gospel to these one-facet understandings of it.

The gospel means many things and has many unique contributions to our lives with God. When we have only one understanding, we unintentionally diminish what the gospel really is. In the end we either settle for a half-gospel or a burst wineskin. And neither of those is very appealing.

The Wine
Using the illustration of wine and wineskins, we then understand wine to be what the gospel actually is. Wineskins are the many different truths and metaphors used

at the gospel means. They hold the gospel within them, but they
and not wine. These wineskins point to the all-important truth,
bu.   skin can point to all of the gospel. The wine is simply more abundant
and bountiful than one skin can hold. And so we need many different skins to
even begin to try to hold the understanding all the ways the wine impacts and
influences our understanding and experience of God and life.

The wine — what the gospel is — really boils down to the story of Jesus. It is
the life, death, burial, and resurrection of Jesus. Most would expand it to include
Jesus' birth and ascension back into heaven as well, but since birth and ascension
are not in every gospel, it's kind of hard to insist on them being at the innermost
core. Still almost all of Christianity has included these in their Creeds, so we
include them here. Below, then, is one way to picture the gospel:

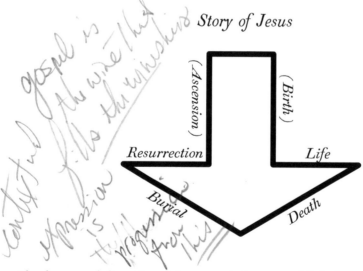

Story of Jesus

The downward direction of the arrow helps us establish the movement of
the gospel. It shows God stepping into history at a specific point and time
in the person of Jesus. This story of Jesus includes his identification as God
and his work of the kingdom, as evidenced in his life and ministry. The story
demonstrates his power over death and evil, and it forecasts his ongoing presence
in the world. In short, Jesus was God. In Jesus, God came into our world. He
lived our life. He showed us how life should be lived. He died. But death did not

defeat him, because he conquered death and lives today. He sustains all things at the right side of the Father. And most importantly, he invites us into his life. This was not just an act of demonstration that showed us what life with God was supposed to be. It was an activity of invitation – of God doing a work that invites us once again to establish covenant with him and to represent his kingdom. In other words, it is God inviting us back into the Garden to recover everything we lost when we rebelled against him.

The Wineskin

When we start to talk about what the (birth and) life and death and burial and resurrection (and ascension) of Jesus means, we immediately need metaphors. So much was regained in Jesus' work on the cross that we could spend all of eternity studying it and still not get to the end of it. And this is what we see happening in the epistles of the New Testament. As people came into contact with the risen Christ, they begin to articulate this living Christ to others. They tell of his life and death. They tell of his resurrection. And they relate it by helping others discover what it all means. So they take pictures of what it means in their day and they begin to relate them to the work of Jesus. But no one picture will suffice to hold all the gospel means.

For instance, as Paul walks into a Roman courtroom, he sees a picture of the gospel. God is the Judge. We deserve to die because we have committed the offense of sin. But Christ has taken our punishment by dying for us. And because Christ has been raised from the dead, he has conquered sin. We can now have right standing with God. We are free from the charges of sin and now given back our life.

Paul uses other metaphors as well. Another metaphor comes from a terrible abuse and tragedy of his day. Kids were being taken from their parents and held for ransom in order to get a payoff. Here Paul again sees a metaphor for the gospel. Satan had kidnapped humanity. Jesus came and lived and died on the cross to pay our ransom. Because he laid down his life and paid the price for our sin, we can now be restored into God's family. We come back into the house and family as children of God.

The writer of Hebrews sees the meaning of the gospel in the Jewish sacrificial system. This sacrificial system provides many different peeks at what the gospel means. First, Jesus is our sacrifice. Our sin has been placed on him. He has died for our sin. As a result, we can now stand in front of God. Even more, we can now enter the Holy of Holies. The place once reserved for the high priest, and for him only once a year, is now accessible for everyone at any time, because Jesus in his life and death and resurrection has torn the veil and invited us in.

As the meaning of the gospel is expounded throughout Scripture, numerous metaphors describe the multifaceted reflection of this great diamond. Here are just a few others to consider:

- Jesus heals us of our disease.
- Jesus returns us into the flock or family as brothers and joint heirs.
- Jesus fully restores our humanity – the image of which had remained but in a tarnished state — and it is now fully available through the work of the second Adam who did right the things the first Adam did wrong.
- Jesus gathers all who have scattered and makes the many one.
- Jesus conquers the kingdom of Satan and re-establishes the rule of God in the world.

The list goes on and on. All of these pictures are wineskins. They hold the gospel. They articulate a particular understanding of what the gospel means. They allow the gospel to be refracted so that different aspects of it shine in the light. And the combination of all of these pictures makes the gospel incredibly beautiful.

These metaphors are not just metaphors, though. They are not just different ways of saying the same truth. Rather, *they are different ways of saying different truths that derive from the same series of events.* So, the gospel does many different things in our life with God. It has implications for our destiny, our relationships, our health, our prosperity, our sacrifice, our situation, our humanity, and our systems. It has implications for everything.

As we step into the gospel, all of these truths and the realities that the truths represent become accessible to us. Now, here is a graphic representation of what it looks like when the point of the gospel opens in the life of a person:

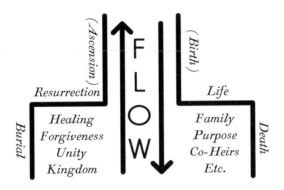

Through the birth, life, death, burial, resurrection, and ascension of Jesus, it is possible for us to have access to the life of God. Who he is has been passed on to who we are. Who we are can be found in who He is. Therefore, our lives are about receiving, surrendering to, and embracing the flow of God's life into our life and our life back into His life. That flow turns all the truth that is uncovered in the different pictures of the gospel into potential realities in our lives as well.

Everyday Gospel

Because the gospel is loaded, and because no single picture can fully demonstrate all that the gospel means, we must work hard to recover *all* of the pictures of gospel within Scripture. In addition, we must also allow the Spirit of God to continue to reveal more pictures and metaphors within our day that can bring to light all that the gospel means. So understanding the gospel is our continual task as archeologists and artists. As archeologists we uncover metaphors of the past. As artists we bring out metaphors in the present. And we should be engaging these tasks every day that we live.

Martin Luther, the great reformer and theologian once said that we should preach the gospel to ourselves every day. In light of what we've just seen, what may have sounded like an exercise in redundancy and routine now sounds more like an exercise of discovery and recovery, as we see the gospel from many different angles and recover more and more of what it should be with every glance.

Already… Not Yet

As we recover the gospel and relate it to our lives, we must also remember that every understanding of the gospel comes with a way in which it is realized. In other words, the really, really good news of the gospel as it relates to life is a reality both now and later. Every metaphor and truth that the gospel relates is, in part, experienced now. But part of the reality can only be fully realized in the future. The scholars and theologians refer to this as already… not yet.

Let's take sin as an example. We are saved when we say yes to Jesus, but everyday we struggle with sin. One day, however, the struggle will be over and Christ's power will be fully realized in our sinless state.

When it comes to healing, the same is also true. At the cross Jesus conquered death. Our disease and illness was cured. Part of this we realize now. Healing today is possible. But no matter what, unless Christ returns at some point we will die. So part of our struggle with death and disease is that we still get sick and it appears the sickness wins. One day, however, no one will be sick. One day there will be no illness. What death took from us, resurrection will restore.

When it comes to prosperity and sacrifice and social out-workings of the gospel, the same pattern holds. Part we experience now. Part we experience not yet.

Our understanding of salvation, then, must be capable of holding these truths. Salvation must be expanded to mean more than one single facet of the gospel, and it must also become a past, present, and future reality. To use Pauline language: we have been saved, we are being saved, we will be saved. Salvation is no longer a single decision. It is a way of life that starts with a single decision but manifests itself in every decision after that.

Redefining Normal

Redefining Normal when it comes to the gospel means realizing that there is more in the gospel than we could ever have imagined. The kingdom has come, is coming, and will come. Restored relationship with God has taken, is taking, and will take place. I am saved, I am being saved, and I will be saved.

Life, health, death, sacrifice, prosperity, significance, meaning, and relationships are and will be different. They will all include both salvation and struggle. What God has started, he will complete, and not even death can keep it from happening. And we get to come along for the ride! Even more, we get to play a role in helping it come into being for both ourselves and others.

But as we join God's gospel mission, we must remember that no single metaphor or articulation of the gospel is sufficient. No single metaphor is worth the devotion of our entire lives. In fact, giving our lives to only one articulation of the gospel will limit our understanding of God, our understanding of his work in Christ, and in the end our mission.

For instance, if the gospel is only about sin and hell, then to be a missionary is only to help people get to heaven. Now the problem is not that this is *inaccurate*; it's that it is *inadequate*.[8] That's because, while this is part of what the gospel means, it's not all that the gospel means. Whole theologies and missionary models have too often been created from only one understanding. And I think it's time for a fuller gospel to be recovered. I'm waiting for a day where missionaries are not just preachers, but doctors and teachers and social workers and yard workers. I'm waiting for a day when people take on these roles not because through them people hear the gospel, but rather because these roles (and others) are the fuller expression of what gospel means. People in these roles become an art gallery of gospel pictures hung in the corridor of everyday life.

Do we settle for Part.

---

[8] Thanks to Aaron Keyes for helping me term this so eloquently in our many discussions about gospel and life with God.

To fully see those things as such, we must recover the gospel that has been lost in the toilets of our half understandings.

Doing so will not happen without criticism. Some might even charge that we are not searching after the gospel at all. But if we persist, we might just recover what others have given up on. *And maybe what we recover will be the other half of the gospel that will change everything.*

CHAPTER
SEVEN

Three-Dimensional Theology

"If we refuse to study theology, it's not that we won't have any
thoughts about God. We'll just most likely have
some very bad ones."
— C.S. Lewis

*"All Scripture is God-breathed
and is useful for teaching, rebuking,
correcting and training in righteousness"
—2 Timothy 3:16*

*H*alf-gospels result in half-theologies. Half-theologies result in half-lives. Half-lives result in half-missions. And half-missions result in a distraught world. So, to recover a full gospel and move toward a fuller mission, we must recover a theological process capable of sustaining it.

When we talk about theology, you are likely tempted to think that this is a chapter only for the experts. That may be based on how some have described theology, but it is not the way theology should be seen. Fisher Humphries, one of the most brilliantly simple men that I have ever had the privilege of learning from, defined theology by saying, "Theology is thinking about God." His dynamic book entitled *Thinking about God* is one of the best resources for building the foundations of a biblical theology that I have ever read. It is brilliant in the way that the most brilliant of things are brilliant — by being simple. But this simplicity comes on the other side of complexity. This simplicity is born from wrestling with complexity, not from avoiding it.

In his magnificent book *Mere Christianity*, C.S. Lewis wrote, "If we refuse to study theology, it's not that we won't have any thoughts about God. We'll just most likely have some very bad ones." Another theologian, A.W. Tozer, said, "The most important thing about a person is what that person thinks about when he thinks about God."

Thinking about God

So what do you think about when you think about God? How do you think about God? As you begin to see God through revelation, you have to wrestle with these questions. This is true because the revelation of God comes to us not like one instant Polaroid picture but more like a puzzle you receive one piece or picture at a time. Theology is how you put the pieces together. And putting the puzzle together can be tricky, especially as you discover pieces of God that seem to be in tension with each other.

You don't have to read the Bible long before you start asking some pretty difficult questions. How can God be both gracious and just? How can Jesus both claim to give those following him life to the max and at the same time tell a rich young ruler to sell everything he owns? These questions, and many more like them, rise to the surface as you begin to discover more about who Jesus is and about the life he chose to live.

As we said before, just because theology is simple doesn't mean you get to it without traveling through the desert of complexity. In fact, often the best theology finds simplicity on the other side of complexity. So I want to invite you into this journey through the desert of complexity for a few moments. The journey may be taxing at first, but in the end I hope it will become simple and give you a better way to put the puzzle together.

One-, Two-, and Three-Dimensional Theology
Many people have proposed many different ways to think about God. My intention here is not to evaluate them one by one. I have tremendous respect for many of these theologians. I have learned from many of them and disagreed with others. This is not the place to dissect their thoughts (or to reveal my own misunderstandings). Rather, what I would like to do is to deal generally with the practice of theology and offer something that has become incredibly helpful for me in my thinking about God.

I want to start this discussion on theology by asking you to think about understanding reality through the experiences of one-, two-, and three-dimensional objects. One-dimensional objects are simply points. Two-dimensional objects connect points into lines and lines into squares or triangles or even circles. Three-dimensional objects connect squares or triangles and circles with other squares, triangles and circles to jump off the page. We've included art of these three dimensions to help you see these differences.

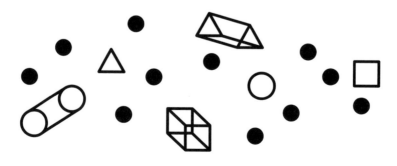

Based on this understanding of reality, I would like to offer some thoughts about how we should think about God. In the past, many of the ways people have thought about God have resulted in theologies that are only one- or two-dimensional. By that, I mean that they are either an endless number of points, or they are built on trying to resolve tension with one-way connections.

When you operate in one dimension, you only have a series of points. These points have no connection to each other and can really become anything we want them to be. They are thoughts about God that function a lot like an inkblot in a Rorschach test. In the end, what we see probably tells us more about ourselves than about the points we see. And so in one-dimensional theology, God becomes anything and everything — and because of that he becomes nothing at all.

When you operate in two dimensions, points connect into lines or circles or squares. A two-dimensional plane highlights the connection between the points. As we connect the dots, we can create objects. And as long as the points can be easily connected, this method is fine. The problem, however, is that some points are more easily connected than others. Points that are harder to connect usually become points that are emphasized less. In the end, those hard-to-connect points are often totally ignored, at least until someone else makes his own theology out of the unconnected points. And so in two-dimensional theologies, God becomes the synergy or resolution of points. Sadly, two-dimensional theologies lose one of our greatest gifts in understanding God: tension.

Let's illustrate these kinds of theology for the visual learners among us. In one-dimensional theology, God is a series of points with no real purpose. There's no puzzle, no picture — just dots. In the end, thinking about God using this approach is kind of pointless, because God can be anything and be any way. This approach to theology usually just ignores any tension that arises. Often in this inkblot way of thinking about God, God tends to start to look like nothing or a lot like ourselves. We remake God in our own image, so to speak.

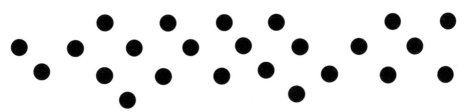

Two-dimensional theology starts to connect the dots. By doing so, this theology can create circles and squares and a host of other shapes. It starts to give us a picture of what God may look like. However, two-dimensional theologies try to resolve tension. So one thing is always prioritized over the other. One set of points takes precedence over other sets of points. God can be one or the other but not both. The best two-dimensional theology can do is to place sets of points it perceives as lesser inside sets of points it perceives as greater. Meanwhile, at its worst, two-dimensional theology disconnects from one set of points entirely.

Two-dimensional theologies too often result in movements that are good but short-sighted. We have either movements of grace or movements of justice, but not both. Wealth submits to poverty, or vice versa. Election trumps free will, or vice versa. We prioritize one picture of God over another. One picture becomes standard; the other becomes neglected. These movements enforce their half-gospels and react to each other by emphasizing what is not said in the other. Each movement champions its own half-gospel and thus its own priorities. Each overcorrects based on the misstep of another and connects the points the other has left out. Often, this leads movements to polarization and even demonization of other movements. And in this polarization and demonization, God is lost.

Two-dimensional theology does make a valuable contribution, because it starts to put pieces of God together. It connects dots into shapes, and by doing so distinguishes itself from the pointless disconnection of one-dimensional theology. *The problem is that it often degenerates and becomes more about resolving tension than about actually reading the Bible.* Too often, those of us who have a two-dimensional theology ignore parts of the Bible that challenge our hierarchal approach. So James submits to Paul. Or the Old Testament is disregarded for the New — even though Jesus said he came not to abolish the law but fulfill it.

Much of the theology of our modern era is two-dimensional. We call them systematic theologies. Again, my intention here is not to diminish their contribution. Two-dimensional theology is better than one-dimensional theology.

Squares are better than dots. And differentiating squares from other shapes is an important theological task. But while these theologies are great in helping us begin to put the puzzle of God together, for me they are limited in their ability to actually describe a higher-dimensional being.

Let me try to explain.

The Man and the World

The story is often told of a little boy who was anxiously awaiting the arrival of his daddy home from work, as little boys often do. So, the boy constantly and continually barraged his mother with one question over and over again: "Mommy, when is daddy coming home?" At 9 o'clock he asked the question. At 9:15 and 9:30 he repeated it. The boy's mother answered the boy each time the same way: "Daddy comes home at 5:00." Still, the boy, full of anticipation but with little awareness for the passing of time, continued to ask his mother. "Mommy, mommy, when is daddy coming home?" He asked at 10:00 and 10:30. He asked at 11:00 and 11:15. All day he asked, and the answer was always the same — "Daddy comes home at 5:00"

Finally, after what seemed like an eternity for both the boy and the mother, 5:00 rolled around. The father's car rolled into the driveway right on schedule. The boy saw the arrival and waited at the door to welcome his daddy with a jump and a hug and a pull. As soon as the door opened, the boy leaped into his daddy's arms and immediately began to make his request: "Let's go play daddy! Please daddy! Let's play daddy! I've been waiting all day daddy. Let's go play daddy!" Of course, the daddy loved his son, but as much as he wanted to play with his son, he wanted to sit in his recliner and catch his breath for just a moment after a rough and tiring day at work.

So the father grabbed the newspaper and plopped down in his recliner with one request to his son. "Son, give daddy five minutes to relax and read the paper, and then I will come play. Just five minutes, then I'll come play." Five minutes went by, and on the dot the boy came back to get his daddy out of the recliner. Again the words, "Let's go play daddy" reverberated from the boy's lips to the daddy's ears. The daddy could hardly believe that five minutes had passed so quickly. So the father begged for another five minutes to relax: "Daddy has had a long day and just needs five more minutes to rest. Just five more minutes." Again time passed, but this time, after just 3½ minutes, the boy was right back at his dad's side, begging his dad to come play.

The dad knew that he couldn't put off his son any longer. So instead of begging for more time, he gave his son a challenge. He took a picture of the world in an advertisement from the paper he was reading and ripped it into 20 pieces. Then he told his son, "Here is a puzzle of the world. When you can get this puzzle all put together, I will come and play." Now, the daddy knew that his son didn't know any geography. He knew that the son had no idea where Afghanistan and Djibouti, Africa, and Venezuela go in relation to each other. While the dad felt a little bad about this trick, he was also relieved that he had bought himself a few more minutes.

You can imagine the father's surprise when his son returned five minutes later with the makeshift puzzle of the world all put together. The father asked his son, "Son, how did you do this? You don't know where Venezuela and Afghanistan and Djibouti, Africa, go. How did you put this puzzle together?" The boy answered, "Well, daddy on the back of that picture of the world was a picture of a man. And once I got the man together, the world came together pretty good too."

Now, most of the time when this old story is told to audiences, the obvious truth drawn from it is that we as people are trying to put our world together, and if we will just focus on the man, then our world will come together pretty good too. The takeaway is to focus on Jesus and let him put our world together. And in a profound and simple way this is true, because Jesus does bring our world together.

But when I tell the story, I often take a minute to challenge the truth found in it. That's because, while focusing on Jesus sounds easier than putting the world together, it's not. In fact, most of us are better at putting the world together than at putting Jesus together. And the disconcerting truth that many of us have discovered as we have tried to put the man together is that Jesus doesn't bring our world together. Instead, he turns our world upside down.

So which is true? Does Jesus bring our world together or flip our world upside down? The answer, of course, is both. But how do we account for this in our theology? Some do this by saying that Jesus does one thing or the other. Others suggest that Jesus brings our world together by flipping it upside down, or vice versa. But I want to suggest a different alternative. Maybe Jesus sometimes brings our world together. And maybe at other times he turns our world upside down. And maybe it is in the rhythm of these two extremes that we find both who He is and how He works. This is why a three-dimensional theology is necessary.

Three-Dimensional Theology

In a three-dimensional theology (or in reality an infinitely multiple theology), we understand characteristics of God not in hierarchy but in tension. We preserve the tension because it is in the tension that God is actually found. The diagram below illustrates this idea.

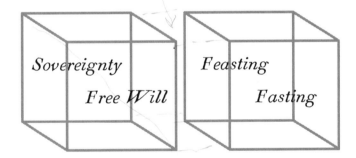

We see here that God's sovereignty doesn't trump God's selfless intuition to give His creation freedom. It's in tension with it. Likewise, God's grace doesn't trump His justice. It's in tension with it. Belief doesn't trump works; instead, faith is found in the tension of them. Fasting doesn't trump feasting, because honor, submission, and allegiance are found in the tension between them. We give proper emphasis on the characteristics in tension by dwelling on God long enough to let both emerge. The Spirit provides the rhythm in which they do. And instead of giving one side priority over the other, we discover that emphasis rotates between both extremes. To see how this might work, examine the cubes

*3. D embracing tension to God
of being*

on the previous page and write down which word is written on the front side of the cube. Then stare for 30 seconds more and see if your perspective changes.

In the rhythm of three-dimensional theology, emphasis replaces priority, because no single emphasis is valued over the other. The value is stabilized between both of them. God is in both extremes. And how we experience God in both extremes in relation to each other is an ongoing work of the Spirit, who directs what our eyes need to see at the present time. The irony is that by embracing the tension instead of resolving it, we cover more ground and allow each emphasis to have a dynamic pull on our life instead dismissing one extreme or the other. By allowing this tension to exist, we move from the world of either/or into the world of both/and. And this world of both/and looks most like Jesus to me.

Consider for a moment the story of when Jesus was asked about whether to pay taxes to Caesar. Make no mistake — this was not just a practical question. It was a theological one. In the polarized, two-dimensional worldview of his day, Jesus had two choices. He could say to pay taxes to Caesar, which would win the approval of one set of theologians and the disapproval of the other set. Or he could say not to pay taxes Caesar and watch the approval and disapproval change sides. But into this world of either/or, Jesus raised the playing field to both/and. He said, "Give to Caesar what is Caesar's and give to God what is God's."[9] In this statement Jesus pulled two disconnected thoughts and ideas together and provided a third way that became the higher ground. Both sides walked away stunned. And as readers we are forever left in a tension that cuts both ways.

Connecting the Squares

The key to this kind of thinking about God is not in how we choose to connect the dots but in how we connect the two squares. Instead of placing them inside of each other, we place them alongside each other and connect them with lines. These four lines provide the basis through which things that seem like they cannot be connected come together. And as they do, they create space for other

---

[9] This story is found in Matthew 22, Mark 12, and Luke 20.

points that look like they can't be connected to be encapsulated in the space of a three-dimensional shape. As they are connected, the two squares move from flat figures to a dynamic three-dimensional object.

In the same way that it is possible for squares to turn into cubes, it is also possible for us to consider thinking about God. We can refer to the four lines that connect things that don't seem to connect as the 4 P's — picture, paradox, poetry and principle. These four vehicles help illuminate truth in ways that systematics alone cannot. In the end, I think the 4 P's help introduce us to a person instead of a mere concept.

If your theology of God is going to be three-dimensional, it has to be more than a series of points or cleverly crafted ideas. It has to be both practical and artistic. It has to be nuanced. It has to leave room for Spirit. And it has to involve tension, because tension is not just good — rather it gives us God.

Let's think about how these 4 P's hold tension.

Picture: This is the P word we use to describe the art of story. If I were to ask you to describe your best friend to me, you might give me some characteristics that would be true of her. But probably at some point you would start telling me stories. Stories demonstrate truth and connect competing truths together. And the more stories you tell me, the more I start to understand who your friend really is.

Principle: This is the P word we use to describe both characteristics of who God is and the way he works. They contain some absolute truths, but they contain many more general and specific truths about God. It is in these general and the specific truths that we find principle's greatest power. Legalism both practically and theologically is the result of turning general and specific truths into absolute ones. Unfortunately, much of fundamentalism in Christianity has resorted to this kind of absolutism as it attempts to combat postmodernism. But neither relativism nor absolutism leads us to God. They only lead us to an artist formerly known as him.

Paradox: Paradox is the art of speaking out of both sides of our mouths. It's not lying. It's often truth in its finest form. It refuses to settle for either/or if the real answer is both/and. By juxtaposing things that seem to be at odds, paradox presents an even higher and better reality. Paradox is the answer to polarization. And in our increasingly polarized society today, it must be something that we learn to speak well in our theologies.

Poetry: Poetry captures truth in emotional and romantic ways that move us past the pettiness of resolution. Its artistic expressions bring insight into God that prose alone cannot. It lifts our spirit and unleashes our imagination.

Redefining Normal

In case you are wondering why you have never read a theology book that looks like this kind of thing that I've been talking about in this chapter, I want to suggest that you have. The Bible is picture and poetry and principle and paradox. It helps us think about God. And it's three-dimensional enough not to resolve the tensions inside it. So I again want to implore you to read the Bible. Don't read the Bible through your theology. Read it *as* your theology. Let it shape your thinking about God. Join in the spirit of Paul as he writes to Timothy that "All Scripture is God-breathed and is useful for teaching, rebuking, correcting and training in righteousness, so that the servant of God may be thoroughly equipped for every good work." (2 Timothy 3:16-17) Don't settle for a small theology put together and reasoned in such a way that it, in the end, gives you a small Bible. Don't try to resolve all of its tensions. Live in them and let them live in you. Let the Bible keep tweaking your thinking about who God is and how God acts, and let the Spirit of God highlight the nuances that you need to lean into at the present moment. As you do, you might just find your world both coming together and being turned upside down.

CHAPTER
EIGHT

3D Glasses

"Discipleship is part discipline"

"And there was evening,
and there was morning
— the first day."
—Genesis 1:5

I love vacation. Vacation is the best six months of my year — just kidding. Someone who has six months of vacation is known as a college student. And unfortunately for me college was a long time ago. Some of you who are college students right now know exactly what I'm talking about. My advice to you is simple. Soak it up. Don't complain about how stressed you are. We all know that college is one big hangout time. It will soon be over, and the rhythms of life will change. But for now you are on an extended vacation, so enjoy it. The rest of us will just settle for our memories and a couple of weeks each year when vacation and life come together. (That is, unless you create a ministry with your best friends and extend college for as long as possible — not that we at Wayfarer would know anything about that.)

Anyway, vacation is a time when we take a break from life and get a chance to catch our breath. One of these moments for me is a week of family vacation that has pretty much become a tradition in our household. During this week, we pack everyone on my wife's side of the family up and head to Myrtle Beach, South Carolina. It's a place that some people refer to as the Redneck Riviera, but we call it our second home.

Every year we do pretty much the same things. We play golf – at least my wife's brother-in-law and I do. We eat big. We relax in the sun and in the lazy river. And on one or two nights during this vacation week, we head over to the local tourist trap known as Broadway on the Beach. This place is a combination of restaurants, shops, rides, and tourist attractions that has a little something for everyone. This past year, it had something that we had heard about but never experienced — an IMAX theatre with a movie in 3D. Now it's not that we had never seen a 3D movie, because nowadays it seems as though 3D movies are everywhere. But this was going to be our family's first 3D movie on a seven-story movie screen.

We loaded up the kids and hit the IMAX, paying the kind of prices you only feel comfortable paying on vacation. We watched *Under the Sea*. In this movie, the ocean literally came to life as we followed the camera for an up-close experience with the underwater sea creatures. And it felt like we were actually in the water with them — at least for those of us who were able to keep our glasses on. (I'm pretty sure that my 3-year-olds saw nothing but a seven-story blur.)

The key to any 3D movie is the 3D glasses that the movie theater gives you before you walk into the show. In a normal theater, these glasses look somewhat normal. But in an IMAX theater, these glasses are ridiculous. They look and feel a bit odd (to say the least).You recognize this first by looking at others who are wearing their glasses and watching the movie. Taking a look around in the theater and seeing others wearing their glasses can be a pretty comical experience. Then it dawns on you that you are one of those people.

So why would anyone do something that looks, feels, and seems odd at best and ridiculous at worst? We do it because, without the glasses, you may see something on the screen, but you don't see the movie the way it was designed to be seen. Without the glasses the movie looks more like a blur than life, but with the glasses everything starts to come into focus, and then the stuff on the screen starts popping up all around you.

The same is true with God. If God is three-dimensional[10], then maybe we too need glasses to help Him come into focus. We may have a three-dimensional theology that helps us understand Him, but to see Him in real life we need a set of lenses. These glasses may feel a little odd at first and may even seem a little ridiculous. But by wearing them, many before us and many of those in the theater of life with us have seen God and life come into focus. Disciples call these 3D glasses the disciplines.

Putting on Your Glasses

There is no getting around it: Discipleship is part discipline. We may not like it,

---

[10] Again, I know that God is more than three-dimensional. We use this idea as an illustration, not as a full description of who God is and what he does.

but it is true. Disciplines are a series of spiritual exercises that disciples do to help them see and hear God in the present. They take some time to get used to. But if we will let them help us, the whole world will come alive with God — 3D style. In the previous chapters, we have talked about the importance of Bible and gospel and theology. These have primarily been expressions of truth with opportunities of Spirit. Disciplines function the exact opposite way. These practices are primarily expressions of Spirit that help illuminate truth. Individually the lenses refract green and red and blue as 3D glasses do. Together they help the truth of God protrude into real life.

The best modern resource that I have encountered to explain the role of disciplines in the life of the disciple is Richard Foster's book *Celebration of Discipline*. In this book, Foster describes the formation of a disciple and the lenses of the disciplines that bring God from blur to life. Below I have listed a short description of some of these disciplines, added some that Foster did not mention, and adapted explanations of each of them to give a brief overview.

Scripture reading: God has revealed Himself to us in Scripture. Scripture shows us who God is, what he is like, and what he expects from us as his followers. It also tells us who God has made us to be. The discipline of Scripture reading, along with prayer, is central to all of Christian living.

Study: Our minds will conform to the things on which they concentrate. Jesus tells us that knowing the truth will set us free. (John 8:32) This discipline will transform us as we take Scripture and slowly read and re-read it. Concentrated study will slowly change our minds to the things of God.

Prayer: Prayer — connecting with God — is the backbone of the Christian faith. Discipleship flows out of a healthy prayer life. It's important to know that we need not be concerned with academic and difficult prayers. God intends for us to practice this discipline of prayer with childlike faith. By both talking to God and listening for God in prayer, the dynamic collision of faith happens as earth reaches toward heaven and heaven is bent toward earth.

Simplicity: The discipline of simplicity helps us as we battle the temptation of materialism. Engaging in this discipline shows us that we truly need only a few things. Our relationship with the living God is what we must focus on. This discipline helps us weed out the unnecessary things in our lives.

Solitude: Many people hate being alone, but solitude has a purpose. The discipline of solitude puts us in position to hear God. It is not natural in this day and age to spend long amounts of time alone focusing on the things of God. That's why we should sometimes make a concerted effort to block out time to be silent in solitude. In the silence, God speaks and dwells, reminding us that he is always present.

Meditation: It seems that the whole world is in a hurry and that our culture is always busy. We are drawn to crowds, noise, and chaos. Meditation helps us break away from this hectic pace to focus our hearts, minds, and souls on God. Meditation is the art of taking a piece of scripture and focusing on it. Picture a cow chewing cud. You swallow the word; it comes up; you swallow it again. The process repeats over and over and over.

Rest: From creation to the 10 commandments, rest is an important part of what God commands us to do. Instead of being slaves to our work, God wants us to take a Sabbath — a day of rest — every week. Other forms of rest are important too, because they give us the physical strength we need to do what God calls us to do when we're awake. No wonder John Ortberg once wrote that sometimes, the most spiritual thing someone can do is to take a nap.

Fasting: Fasting is a discipline that uses the absence of something to remind us of the presence of God. When we fast, our spiritual senses are awakened, and they become more sensitive to God's presence. There are various types of fasts, not just food, and we should be careful to use fasting in healthy way. But whatever form they take, in these moments of going without, we allow ourselves to be truly full.

Service: This is a very practical discipline that puts the needs of others in front of our own. True Christian service is not done for show, but for the other person. In doing so, we imitate and follow Jesus, the greatest servant of all time. We find that being last is actually first and that in becoming small we also become mature.

Celebration: Celebration may not seem like a spiritual discipline, but it has always been an important part of what it means to follow God. In the Old Testament, the Israelites celebrated what God had done for them through a series of feasts. In our day, we too need to take time to celebrate what God has done and will do.

Remember, these disciplines are expressions of Spirit that lead us to truth. They move God from a book to life. They help God be less like something we talk about in the past and instead Someone we experience in the present. This present-tense experience of God speaking to us and indwelling in us comes to us in many different ways. I have only listed a few. But what we experience must lead us to and be interpreted by truth. In this way both revelation and inspiration hold hands thanks to the perspiration of discipline, and this perspiration in an almost awkward way gives our souls the rest they desperately need.

Now Focus

It's easy to think that life is a race. We run so fast from Point A to Point B that we forget that the journey is just as important as the destination. We have to remind ourselves that God is not someone to whom we are trying to get. Life is not something at which we arrive. No, God is already here, and life is a series of choices we make in the present. We need only to stop for a few minutes and let life and God come into focus. We will need to put on our glasses for this to happen. But if we do, God and life will become less of blur and more like the protruding reality they are. So part of engaging in disciplines means setting a rhythm for life that leaves room for reading and study and solitude and service and celebration. We meditate on God's goodness. And as we put the disciplines into practice, we will begin to see work and relationships as an expression of rest instead of the other way around.

God established this rhythm for life back in the garden. Each separate expression of creation was separated by a pregnant phrase: "And there was evening, and there was morning — the ___ day." (First, second, etc.) This is interesting if you think about it. It's not the way we normally think days move. Most of the time, when we think of a day, we think of morning coming before evening, not evening coming before morning. But maybe the Bible knows something we don't. Maybe God knows that *we were meant to work from rest, not rest from work*. Maybe we were meant to breathe before we live, because it is in the breathing that we catch life. "And God breathed into man's nostrils the breath of life and man became a living soul." (Genesis 2:7)

semi-circle

Disciplines help us breathe. By breathing we rest. In rest we see. In seeing we become. In becoming we live. And we live in 3D.

From Believing to Becoming

We started this journey of revelation with a startling question. We said that when it comes to pursuing truth, the question was not "Will we find it?" but "Can we handle it?" God wants to be discovered. But when we find Him, we must be willing to change. The Bible shows us who God is. The gospel shows us what we can be. Theology helps us hold together the tension. And disciplines create the atmosphere in which we become who we were meant to become. They help God come into life — not just life in general, but into our lives.

Seeing God and trying to become like him will be a constant rhythm of embrace and surrender. When we see who God is, we embrace Him. By embracing Him we surrender ourselves. In surrendering ourselves we change. And as we change, we become more like who God is and who we were meant to be.

Being a disciple is not just believing a set of truths about God. It is letting what we believe about God change who we are becoming with God. So if we stop just believing and start becoming, we show that we can indeed handle the truth.

Redefining Normal

We don't practice disciplines to please God. We practice disciplines to breathe God. So stop a minute and take a deep breath. Just as you breathe in and out, you live inside and out. You are more than what you do. You are more than what you accomplish. You are a soul, and souls need to breathe. Souls need to see. It's good to see you with your glasses on. Yes, you look a little funny. But you are starting to look alive.

SECTION
THREE

The 864

*T*he area code for my community in Greenville, South Carolina, is 864. If you are reading this book in America, you too have an area code. You too have numbers that designate your community. In Birmingham, Alabama, that area code is 205. On the Space Coast of Florida, the area code conveniently is 321.

Area codes remind us that we live in communities. In these communities are all kinds of people. The question is whether you and I are letting this community of people give us life and whether we are offering our lives to the people we find ourselves in community with. Redefining normal discipleship includes both.

Discipleship is part information, but it is also part imitation. It is revelation, but it is also relationship. It is content, but it is also community. This is because as much as discipleship can be taught, it must also be caught.

Everywhere I go it seems like people are looking for community. But community is not something you find. Community is something you engage. You live in a community. You work in a community. You go to school in a community. You go to church in a community. You are part of this community. But are you engaging it?

Now it is true that some of the people inside your community have potential to lead you away from Christ. But many others have potential to lead you toward Christ. And you have the opportunity to lead many others toward Christ. So how can we engage community as a means of becoming a disciple?

The way we engage community for discipleship is by engaging people. Every person needs someone to learn from. Every person needs someone to learn with. Every person needs someone to teach. Communities are full of these kinds of people. And if we will let these kinds of people into our lives, they will help us become disciples of Jesus. We simply cannot become disciples on our own. We cannot become who Jesus would be if he were us without help. And we cannot do it without helping others in the meantime. Walking with others is part of the way that we become our true selves and begin to resemble Christ with our lives.

The last section of our journey of Redefining Normal primarily concentrated on the left side of the Equation of Resemblance – namely how we begin to understand who Jesus was and what Jesus did. (We expanded this to God as well.) This section will help us begin to bridge the gap to the right side of the equation. By seeing how others have lived and are living, we can begin to picture what our lives could look like and how they might resemble Jesus. And as we help others begin to do the same, God matures in us what was planted in us by others.

$$\frac{5}{10} = \frac{X}{30}$$

Are you ready to stop looking for community and start engaging the community you find yourself in? Opportunities to be discipled and disciple others are all around you. Let's see how this might work.

CHAPTER
NINE

The Revolutionary Road

"We are like dwarfs standing on the shoulders of giants"
— Peter of Blois

*"Even if you had ten thousand
guardians in Christ,
you do not have many fathers,
for in Christ Jesus I became your father
through the gospel.
Therefore I urge you to imitate me."*
—1 Corinthians 4:15-16

*F*or a large part of my life, my biggest life dreams revolved around the soccer field (or as my friends from England might say, the football pitch). I loved playing soccer and even had the chance to play on scholarship at a small college in southern Florida. I enjoyed becoming a better player, and I loved coaching others to do the same. Thankfully, in college I had the opportunity to do both.

Our coach's philosophy was that part of becoming a better player happened by coaching others. So we spent much of our time every offseason coaching local high school teams. In the summer we often traveled around the country coaching and teaching kids at soccer camps.

One summer, my buddies and I had the opportunity to work a soccer camp called Joe Machnick's No. 1 Keeper and Striker Camp. I enjoyed my time helping the kids. But what I learned most that summer was *how* to coach. Learning this helped me understand how my best coaches had helped me, both in soccer and in life.

This camp functioned under a simple philosophy. With every drill through which we led campers, we were to first tell them what we were hoping to accomplish and how the drill worked. Then we as coaches would show campers how to do it by running a demo for them to watch. The demo would show the drill completed at the highest level so the kids got a picture in their minds of what they were trying to imitate. So we as college athletes did the drill ourselves as part of our coaching assignments. After the demo, we invited the players into the drill. As they participated in the drill, we stepped in and pointed out places they were succeeding and celebrated them. We also pointed out places they could improve and helped them do so. Finally, we linked the drill to a scrimmage of some kind so that the drill made the transition from practice to the game.

Now, not every practice had as clean of a transition as I have written down. But this was the intention. The progression was simple: Tell them → Show them →

in in → Celebrate and help them as they try to do it themselves → Link
ney are doing to a game situation.

The reason I bring up this pattern is that it's not just the best way to coach soccer.
I think it might also be the best way to become a disciple and make a disciple.
The people who impacted my life the most for the kingdom of God are people
who did this for me. They didn't always know this pattern was what they were
doing. The process wasn't always clean and tight. But it's what they did. And
because they did it, they have helped me look more like Christ.

This same progression is also what Jesus did. The gospels tell the stories of
Jesus helping his disciples see and engage God and his life in their lives. He told
them about God. He showed them how to relate to him at the deepest levels.
He invited them in. He celebrated them when they got it right. He helped them
when they got it wrong. And he sent them out to do the same with others in the
game of life. Because of Jesus' example, this process has lived on.

So as we begin looking at the pattern of discipleship in our lives, we come to the
first truth that *becoming a disciple means learning from a disciple*. It means allowing
someone into your life to mentor or coach you in the things of God. It means
admitting that you need help and looking to those a little ahead of you in the
process to find it.

Revolutionaries or Rebels

Life with a mentor is so important because, without one, we will most likely
mistake revolution for rebellion. Both rebels and revolutionaries see the same
problems in the world and, to be frank, even in the church. Both sense a kind
of righteous indignation. But rebels know only how to deconstruct. They forge
their identity only by what they are moving against. Because of this, they have
nowhere to move once they have deconstructed. They tear down things that need
to be torn down, but don't know what to do with the rubble they create. So in
the end, they become deconstructionists who find meaning in life in destructive
ways.

Revolutionaries are different. They too know that something is wrong. They too know that something must change. But they also know that this change means more than deconstruction. Deconstruction is only as good if it gives way to reconstruction. So revolutionaries move from what is, to what could be, and in the end to what will be. This kind of revolutionary sight or vision many times comes as the result of taking time to learn from the insight of others, especially those who are down the road a little farther.

That's why I think the most powerful thing that I could do to help you understand how this works is to tell you a few stories of how this has worked in my life. In other words, I want to invite you to see the way that the life of Jesus has been passed to me. As I tell you these stories, I hope it helps you to identify how Jesus' life has been best passed to you, or at least to identify how it might happen even if it hasn't happened yet. I want you to identify these people so that you can resist the temptation of becoming a mere rebel when God is asking you to become a revolutionary.

As you'll see in the following stories, my life mentors come from lots of different life stages and perspectives. But each of them showed me how to become like Christ. As I imitated their life, I embraced more of Christ's life.

Mom and Dad

To be honest, I almost feel guilty starting here, because I know that many of you reading this book have not had the privilege of finding Christ's life in the lives of your parents. For some of you, your parents have been a source of far more hurt than help. They have showed you the anti-Christ life far more than the Christ life. But as I tell this part of my story, I hope you can hear what should be and, even more, what could be for your children. I know God can heal your wounds, and even more, He can make you a wounded healer.[11]

---

[11] Henri Nouwen's term

My mom and dad were not perfect, but they were and are Christ followers. Ever since I can remember, they have told me about Christ. They have showed me Jesus in their lives. They have invited me in as they processed what it means to be Christian. And they have helped me embrace Christ in my life. They have become both my biggest fans and my greatest help. Much of the ministry that God has used me to do has its roots in the path on which they started me.

While there are many stories I could tell you about my mom and dad, none looms larger than the way they showed Christ to my brother and me at one of the most critical times in our childhood. I was 12 at the time, and my brother was 10. We had grown up in a house and community where from the time we were born we had heard about life and faith in Jesus. But at this point in our lives, my dad began hearing the voice of God tell him that it might be time for us to move. This wasn't a random move or an upgrade for a better job. It was a move that resulted from a sense of calling. Until this point my dad had been a physical education teacher at a Christian university. But as God began to speak to my dad, my dad began to sense a call to pastor a church. This call would mean a drastic upheaval for our family, both in what we did and where we lived.

My mom and dad knew just how big this life decision would be not just in their life but in the lives of my brother and me. So they invited us into the process. They invited us to hear God with them. They invited us to pray. They invited us to seek. They invited us to evaluate. Faith that we had talked about was now being demonstrated, and we were invited to be a part of it. In the end, we did move. It was one of the hardest times in my young life. I didn't fully get it all at the time. But I did see God work — even miraculously at times. And as I look back on those moments that now stand 25 years in the past, I know that my mom and dad helped me enter faith through this moment and others like it.

This moment was not an isolated instance for my parents. Over the years I have watched my mom and dad continue to listen to God. I have watched them change everything. I have watched them continue to learn. And they have continued to invite me and now my family into the process. Now I am doing the same with my family, and I hope that my wife Kim and I can live up to what has been handed down to us[12].

Mr. Jim

Every child, every student, and every young adult needs an adult other than his or her parents to speak into their lives and show them Jesus. Mr. Jim was the first to do this for me. He and his wife were my parent's friends. Mr. Jim and his wife didn't have kids at the time, so we became his kids. He taught our Sunday School class. He took us to McDonald's while our parents were at choir practice. He was the most creative storyteller I have ever been around. He knew how to make the Bible come alive. He told us the stories of the Bible and even a bit of theology so beautifully that somehow I knew what the Pentateuch was when I was 6.

Mr. Jim also helped my dad coach our soccer team. He didn't really even know how to play soccer, but we were only 10, so he could still help. He went to our games. He celebrated our victories. And in the process of life, he showed me Jesus. Lots of my knowledge of God goes back to a little Sunday School room where the guy who helped coach my soccer team and took us every week to McDonald's told us about God and Jesus. Lots of my teaching and storytelling has its roots in how he taught us.

Brent and Dolly Thomas

Brent and Dolly Thomas brought grace, generosity, and extravagance to my life. Each of these qualities I now see in Jesus. They were about 60 years old when we met. I was a teenager struggling to live faithfully as a pastor's kid. Being a pastor's kid is tough. You live in a glass house. Often your family is underpaid. You definitely get to see the dark side of church life.

Brent and Dolly knew this, I think. So they saw it as their mission in life to spoil me and my brother. They became our third set of grandparents. They provided for us in ways my parents were unable to. They overpaid us for chores we did at

---

[12] Thankfully, this is not just the story of my life. It is also the story of my wife's life. Her parents too invested in her life deeply and invited her into the process. I wanted to take a moment here to thank them also for what they have passed to her.

their house. They even bought me my first car — a light blue Ford Escort. Mr. Thomas introduced me to golf and showed me how to play. He let us hit his new drivers. He let us drive his classic car. Brent and Dolly even became the volunteer youth directors at our church for a while.

Neither of them had a seminary degree. Neither of them were the most dynamic teachers in the classroom. But they showed enough love, not just to me and my brother but everyone in our group, that we all wanted to be like them. So we did whatever they suggested. They didn't have spiked hair or cool tattoos, but they loved us in ways that showed us Jesus. And as they showed us Jesus in their actions, we became more like Jesus in return. Today I know that Brent and Dolly played a huge role in making sure that I was a pastor's kid who actually kept my faith instead of abandoning it.

Danny Goodman
This story may be the hardest for me to tell. Even as I begin typing it now my heart hurts just a little bit.

Danny Goodman was the most Christian man I have ever known. I first met him when I was a student in college. I was taking New Testament Hermeneutics as an elective for my religion minor at Palm Beach Atlantic University. He was a new professor teaching and still working in lieu of his of Ph. D. He was only a few years older than us. And he was one of the best teachers I have ever had. I had no idea my life was about to be changed when I walked into his classroom.

Every college has professors who know the material and professors who know the students. Few have professors who know both. But usually on every campus there is one who does. You know this professor because of the long line of students that follow him or her around campus even when they aren't required to do so. At PBA Danny Goodman was this professor.[13] Danny engaged our

---

[13] Let me give a quick shoutout here to Dr. Myers and Dr. Wharton too. These guys did in the business school what Danny did in the religion department. As a Business Management major, I spent many afternoons in their offices, and they too helped me toward Christ.

classroom with a dynamic I had never encountered before. He knew how to make us think. He challenged our paradigms and introduced me to a side of Christ and his kingdom that I am still unearthing today. And he invited us into his life in the process.

We continued our classroom discussion long after the class bell had rung. Often we went from Hermeneutics to lunch and sat down over pizza to discuss the implications of his latest lecture. He engaged me so much that I learned to mimic his mechanics and tone with my own presentations. And he set my spirit free in a way no other professor had. I'm pretty sure that the reason I'm still a learner today is because of Danny Goodman.

Unfortunately, just a few years ago Danny Goodman — or Dr. Daniel E. Goodman, to use his professional title — died. He was just 40 years old. His funeral was one of the spiritual highlights of my life. There I heard his wife Barbara and sons Daniel and Dillon tell the story of a man who was as good a dad and husband as he was a teacher. I watched hundreds of other students testify to the way Dr. Goodman had helped them with faith and intellect. I saw in that moment what I hope my life would one day be.

Dr. Goodman said that the best evaluation of our teaching is not the answers our students can give us but the way they choose to live their lives. He measured his own teaching by saying that the quality of our teaching is best measured in the quality of peers we create.

Long after I graduated from PBA, I still found my way back to Danny's office from time to time. Each time I met with him he continued to show me Jesus. He met me with a genuine love and respect that I was not due. He even championed my accomplishments as if they had exceeded his own. For this and so much more, Danny Goodman still remains someone that I am trying to imitate. Because the more I look like Danny, the more I also begin to look like Jesus.

Dr. Robert Smith Jr.
I thought no one would ever be able to help me learn about God like Danny

Goodman had — until I met Dr. Smith. Fortunately for me, Dr. Smith came
to teach Preaching at Beeson Divinity School at the exact time I was entering
seminary there. I had no idea of the deep levels of impact that this African-
American scholar and pastor would have on my life. To this day he is one of my
fathers in ministry.

I took 20 hours of classes from Dr. Smith in seminary. I took that many hours
not because I had to, but because I didn't care what I was learning as long as he
was teaching. Once I had him for Preaching class, I wanted him for every class.
He was the kind of teacher who, like Danny Goodman, was a student's professor.
Often Dr. Smith would meet me in a hallway or elevator and tell me that he had
just been speaking to the Father on my behalf. Chills would shoot up my spine
because I knew he wasn't lying, and I was pretty sure he had a direct connection.

Dr. Smith talked to us about engaging the whole person with our preaching –
the head, the heart, and the hands. He called us his sons and daughters, and he
was a great dad. He too set my spirit free and showed me how to speak not just
a message but a Word. Even now, if you hear me preach, you'll hear how much
of who I am as a communicator came from Dr. Smith. Listen close, and you may
even hear this white boy try to whoop just a little at the end of one of my talks.
And more than just imitating Dr. Smith in my presentation, I can only hope I
imitate him in revelation. Maybe, just maybe, on my best day I can live up to
what was poured into me by this deep spiritual father.

Carl and Betty Kresge

Carl and Betty Kresge are my wife's grandparents. They also happen to be some
of the most generous people I know. They are leaving our family a legacy to live
up to with their lives. Carl was the vice president of Eastern Industries as a young
man, but that was really only his title. His real passion was his relentless pursuit
of helping humankind, both as an organizer and a fund raiser for important
causes in every city he has lived in. Even now, this 86-year-old man spends his
Fridays delivering meals to people who would probably not eat if he didn't make
his way to their homes. He walks our neighborhood twice a day. He knows
everyone, and everyone knows him.

Betty, my wife's grandmother, is the matriarch of my wife's side of the family. She loves us and our kids in a thoughtful and substantial way like few people I have ever come across. Very few days go by where we do not receive a card or word from her. She remembers every birthday and every anniversary. She plays with my kids and gives them popsicles. And she prays for us daily.

Carl and Betty too have blessed my life in ways that go beyond what I deserve. Today they are showing me what finishing life well looks like. Their legacy lives on in my wife's parents and I hope, one day, in Kim and me.

Mike Breen

My current mentor is Mike Breen. Mike is the founder and leader of 3-Dimensional Movements[14], an organization based in Pawleys Island, South Carolina. He is a global leader and apostolic voice for my generation. I met Mike just about two years ago. I was in a very tough time of life and ministry, and I found in Mike something to imitate. I wrote the first draft of this book as I spent a sabbatical in Pawleys Island learning from Mike and his team. In him and them, I have found one of the most authentic expressions of a genuine faith community that I have ever seen.

This book owes a great deal to Mike. He is the one who opened my eyes up to the idea of information and imitation. Our relationship is only just beginning, but in the year and a half that I have been learning from Mike, I find myself more deeply understanding and moved by the person of Jesus. Both in his teaching and in his life, Mike is opening my eyes to what movemental leadership looks like for the kingdom. He has a combination of deep theology and charisma that I have rarely come across. When I look at him, he shows me what I could become. So I am following his footsteps and picking up his dust on my clothes. And as I do so, I am becoming more like Jesus.

The 3DM logo on this book marks the merge not just of Mike's influence on my

14 www.weare3dm.com

life but now also on my and my team's ministry. Wayfarer is merging with 3DM as a continued expression of mentoring as part of discipleship. So even today I'm practicing this kind of pattern with my life.

Mentors from Afar

These are just a few of my stories. I don't have time to tell you all them. My life is indeed indebted to these people and others whose names have not been included in this list — people like the Floras and the Milligans, the Mansurs and the Taylors, Rick Ousley and Randy Hall, the Cannons and the Lyles, Steve Keyes and Charlie Boyd, Caz McCaslin, and many more.

I could also include as mentors a long list of authors who have mentored me from afar with their books. I have included a bibliography at the end of this book in Appendix A so that you too might be mentored by them. Through their words on paper, they too have entered my life and shown me how to resemble Christ. The words in this book I'm sure in some way have been spawned by theirs. I claim these words and ideas as my own just as they have done with their books. And I can only hope that this book and the others that are still to come might serve someone the way theirs have served me.

Living life with a mentor has for me become the road to revolution and not rebellion. It has given me insight I would not have been able to see with only my own eyes. It has shown me what life with Christ looks like from a few steps ahead. And by giving me someone to imitate, it has initiated Christ's life in me.

Redefining Normal

I hope by now you understand my point. There are lots of people in your community to learn from. Some of the people I have told you about were placed in my life. Some of them I pursued. Most of them were a little of both. Now, I too have become one who, as the medieval theologian Peter of Blois described, "stands on the shoulders of giants." And because I have had shoulders to stand on, I am a little taller and can see a little more of what life could be.

So why don't you join me on this revolutionary road? Your story will not look identical to mine, but it could resemble it. If you will just look around and find someone to learn from, you might be surprised just what kind of access they will give you to their lives. And who knows what they might mean to you becoming like Jesus? You can't follow Jesus on your own. So find someone worth imitating and rearrange your life to get in on theirs. It may be inconvenient at first, but it's the shortest way to looking like Jesus, because by imitating their life, you are really imitating Christ's life.

In case that makes you a little uncomfortable, listen to what Paul wrote to the church at Corinth: "I am writing this not to shame you but to warn you as my dear children. Even if you had ten thousand guardians in Christ, you do not have many fathers, for in Christ Jesus I became your father through the gospel. Therefore I urge you to imitate me. For this reason I have sent to you Timothy, my son whom I love, who is faithful in the Lord. He will remind you of my way of life in Christ Jesus, which agrees with what I teach everywhere in every church." (1 Corinthians 4:14-17)

In the New Testament we find this imitation happening all the time. Timothy was not Paul's biological son, but Paul was Timothy's spiritual father. There are fathers and mothers out there for you too. And in order to follow Jesus and redefine normal, you need to find them and get in on their lives. So let them tell you and show you and invite you in. Because you just might find that in the end you have been with Jesus.

That, my friends, is revolutionary.

CHAPTER
TEN

Community Chest

"When I confess to my brother
it is as if I am confessing to Christ Himself."
— Dietrich Bonheoffer

*"These are the names of the twelve
apostles: first, Simon (who is called
Peter) and his brother Andrew;
James son of Zebedee, and his brother John;
Philip and Bartholomew; Thomas and Matthew
the tax collector; James son of Alphæus, and
Thaddæus; Simon the Zealot and Judas
Iscariot, who betrayed him."
—Matthew 10:2-4*

*E*veryone needs a mentor. But learning *from* someone is not enough.

Everyone needs someone to learn *with*. This is because following Jesus is a team sport. It may start with a call to us individually, but that call will always lead us to others. In other words, while following Jesus may be personal, it is never private.

We all need people around us who we can join in our everyday discovery of Christ. We need friends that become family and family members that become friends to help us see God as he is despite our personal blind spots. Without the team, we will too often fashion God in our own image. It takes the passions and sensitivities of others traveling alongside us to tweak our unprepared and default responses to God.

Personally, this idea of team travel is something I lean into. In fact, it's something that I have grown to love. I love it selflessly because of the great joy that comes from helping others see Jesus more clearly. I also love it selfishly because of what happens in me when others help me do the same. And I think, given a little time, you will learn to love it too.

The African Nightmare

Almost every Christ-follower I have ever talked to has had the same dream — or should I say nightmare. I call it the "African Nightmare." Now this description is not intended to demean my African brothers and sisters. I only call this the African Nightmare because I think Africa is the place most Americans think about when they think about the location on our planet that is as far away from home as it could possibly be. (If you are living in Africa and reading this book, then maybe you would call this your American Nightmare.)

This dream feels as real to us as the other recurring nightmares we have: the dream about going to school or work without any clothes on, the dream about getting in a fight with your spouse or significant other that feels so real you wake up mad, the dream about finding yourself about to take an exam that you have forgotten to study for. For some of us, that last dream still happens even though we've been out of school for years. For others of us, that last dream was actually real life.

This is how the African Nightmare goes: We think that when we say yes to Christ, it means that we are saying no to everyone around us. We're pretty sure that God is out to ruin our lives. This half-constructed theology of God makes us think that God's greatest desire is to send us by ourselves to somewhere like Africa and leave us there on own. Faithful Christianity then looks like a game of Survivor in an African jungle, as we are left all by ourselves with only the occasional visit from God to let us know that we are what real Christianity is all about. The African Nightmare can have different variations, but it's the same dream.

Too often, this dream or hunch keeps us from following Christ with all of our heart. The fear of being alone drives us away from God.

But maybe we have it all backward. Maybe, instead of the fear of being alone driving us away from God, the fear of being alone should actually drive us toward God. That's because God is the author of community. He is community (Father, Son and Holy Spirit). And his followers follow in community. God has not tried to isolate us. Isolation comes from another unseen force — Satan himself.

I know this because I've discovered an ironic thing about the African Nightmare. Now I actually know people who are missionaries and Christ followers in Africa — and they are not alone.

Life Together

All this is why I can now say that one of the biggest discoveries of my Christian life is that God was not calling me to live my life alone. The last 20 years of my life have given testimony to this in the best of ways. In these years of living life with others and discovering Jesus together, I have laughed more than I ever thought I would and have cried more too. I discovered more, celebrated more, and sacrificed more than I ever could have imagined. It has been the most fun thing I have ever done, even though it has come at some of the greatest cost I have ever paid. But one thing I can say with conviction is that in surrendering to follow Christ I have never really been alone.

Now this doesn't mean there haven't been moments where I haven't felt like I was alone. And it doesn't mean I have avoided moments where it felt like following God was costing me my friendships. But what it does mean is that I have discovered that God wants me to live my life with others as much as, if not more than, I want to. And in this journey with others, I have become more like Christ.

This journey first started coming into fruition for me in college. In high school, I had many acquaintances but few real friends. Those few friends were key to my spiritual formation, but because they were so few in number, in some ways they represented my biggest fear — that following Christ meant having few friends.[15] I have come to realize that this had more to do with the particular brand of Christianity my family and I found ourselves in at the time than it did with Christ himself. College, on the other hand, became the place where I started to move out of my fear of following Christ alone and started experimenting with my deepest hope that following Christ could and should be done with others.

What I found was that many other people were hoping for the same thing. So college for me was a journey in community— and a large one at that. It was a community filled with all kinds of interesting people. And in this group, we helped each other look more like Christ. Gathered in community and life on the street of Mango Promenade, just down the street from Palm Beach Atlantic

---

[15] One of these key friends for me was Andy Milligan. Andy and I walked through the shadows of high school together, each helping the other follow Christ. Now, ironically, Andy is headed to Africa in a social experiment to help feed children suffering from malnutrition and provide local jobs at the same time. And he is doing it because as he does so, he is following Christ. We are both Christ followers, recovering from the unfortunate force of fundamentalism in both of our lives.

University, we affectionately referred to ourselves as The Mango Men. Our athletic expression for student-body domination was called The Dutchboyz. But in our work and study and play, something was awakening beyond the cheesy names we called ourselves.

It was one of the best seasons of my life. We were learning how to become disciples of Jesus together. Somewhere between the movies and the meals and the moments we shared together, Christ emerged in our midst. We saw Him in each other's reflections, even if only hazily sometimes. The amount of ministers and ministries that have emerged from this group is staggering. God really was in our midst (even though at times we could have been accused of pushing the line a little bit) and even more, he was the author of it.

This movement continued for me in seminary. In the hallowed halls of Beeson Divinity School and the creative courtyard known as Student Life, this way of life that I discovered in college continued to grow. We worked together. We studied together. We lived in the same apartment complex. We called this little society Melrose Place after the hot drama of the 1990s that showed a group of friends living in the same apartment complex and doing life together. (We still hadn't gotten any better with names). More Christ followers, ministers, and ministries emerged from this group. There are people from this extended family of friends who now live literally all over the country and the world making significant impact for Christ. This has happened not because we found a secret formula but because Christ again was really in our midst as we led and followed each other.

In his book *Life Together*, Dietrich Bonheoffer makes this statement, "When I confess to my brother, it is as if I am confessing to Christ himself." It is a testimony to the power and presence of Christ in brotherhood. It is even more powerful if you begin to imagine that confession is not just repentance of sin (the negative portion of confession) but also the belief of what could be and really is (the positive portion of confession, as when we make a confession of faith). So, as we repent and believe with each other, we are doing so as if we were doing this with Christ. Life together, then, is a series of repent and belief conversations that we have with each other. It happens both planned and spontaneously. It happens repeatedly with intimate and close friends and even sometimes starts to include our acquaintances. And as we converse, we lead and follow each other as we walk beside each other to Christ.

Wayfarer

The greatest expression of this idea of learning together for the past 10 years for me has been the community of learning that known as Wayfarer. Some see us as a ministry, but that is not really who we are. We are really a community on a mission. We describe ourselves by saying, "The creative conspiracy of deep personal friendship and an insatiable desire to learn makes Wayfarer a different kind of team. By melding practical theology with media technology, we hope to design collisions that awaken lives to rediscover Christ."

This is not just something we put on paper. It is actually true. Every day we go to work and play in an act of discovering and learning to imitate Christ. We work hard together and vacation together. We live life with each other and raise our kids together. We are both close friends and mission partners. And it is has been the best journey of my life. David and Courtney Reichley, Chris and Audrey Brooks, Chad and Wendy Norris, Robert and Lindsay Neely, Blake and Kim Berg, Dawn Sherill, Allen and Sharis Kirkland, Aaron and Megan Keyes, David and Lauren Walker, Jennifer Johnsey (now Jennifer Britt), and last (but most certainly not least) my wife Kim Rhodes have all been life partners in this journey. Each of them has helped me know Christ better and better represent him with my life. It has been the great joy of my life to follow Christ with these heroes. And even though some of them have now moved to a different street address, we will always be life partners in Christ.

The Disciples

In the Bible, the group of Jesus followers living life together and each helping the other imitate Christ were known as disciples or apostles. Here is the list we find in Matthew 10: "These are the names of the twelve apostles: first, Simon (who is called Peter) and his brother Andrew; James son of Zebedee, and his brother John; Philip and Bartholomew; Thomas and Matthew the tax collector; James son of Alphaeus, and Thaddaeus; Simon the Zealot and Judas Iscariot, who betrayed him." (Matthew 10:2-4)

Each name represented a particular human being with particular strengths, weaknesses, insights, and ministry potential. Most of them did things they never could have done on their own because they did life together. Others like Paul and Timothy and Mary Magdalene later came into their midst. The New Testament is a testimony to their way of life together in Christ.

We all can be included on a list of disciples. We just have to choose to do life with them. We can all invite others to help us learn and grow. This learning may take place as we sit in classes or go to work together. It also may be the kind of learning that happens in the everyday activities of life. You might raise your kids together and go to lunch together. It might happen as you go on vacation together.

At the back of this book in Appendix B, I have taken a moment to share my list of fellow disciples with you and write a few sentences about them. I include it in this book not to brag but to show you an example of what a group of disciples on journey together might look like today. I also do this so that you might be inspired to find your own band of disciples and spend your lives changing the world together. So if you're interested, turn and read about who these people are. If not, no worries. I'm more concerned with you finding your own group than reading about mine.

Redefining Normal

If you have traveled with me this far in this chapter, then maybe you have begun to see why I enjoy my life so much. I enjoy it because I am traveling with others who make me so much more like Christ than I could be on my own. I am a disciple of Christ, but I am also part of a group of disciples who are discipling each other together. And we are having the time of our lives. The good news is that this is not just my opportunity. It can be yours too.

You were meant to do life with other people. This is part of the imitation process.

As you lead and follow each other, your rough edges become smoother, and your places of brokenness become beautiful again. This certainly has happened to me. And for that I thank all those, both named and unnamed, who continue to speak into my life. Based on my testimony, I invite you to do the same.

CHAPTER
ELEVEN

Water Works

"If you want to run fast, run alone. If you want to run long,
run with someone."
— Jenaraj D. G., East India Director, Compassion

*"Then Jesus went around teaching
from village to village.
Calling the Twelve to him,
he began to send them out two by two
and gave them authority over impure spirits."
—Mark 6:6-7*

So far in this section on imitation, we have talked about people to learn from and people to learn with. These people are in our communities just waiting to be engaged. And each of them to some degree or another has a resemblance of Jesus in them. As we learn to be like them through imitation, we at the same time learn to be like Jesus. But finding people to learn from and people to learn with is not the end of this people movement. There is something more.

Everyone needs someone to teach. We all need someone to invest Christ's life in. We all need someone to whom we can pass our insights and revelation of God. Each of us needs someone we can help along the way. Part of becoming a disciple is making one.

Just trying to become a follower of Jesus will not get you to Jesus. It will give you the right goal. It will even get you a large part of the way. But inherent to becoming like Jesus is helping someone else become like Jesus. It's not an outcome of being a disciple; rather it is part of the process.

If there is one part of the discipleship process that I would say I have been working on the last few years and am working on the most right now, it is this one. This may seem kind of odd for those of you that know me, because most of you know me because of my teaching. But in this chapter, I'm not just talking about teaching from a stage to convey information, as I often do. Rather, I'm referring to a kind of teaching that allows people to have access to your life. This kind of teaching invites others to come in and learn to do what you are doing.

In the past, I have been pretty good at learning from others. I've been really good at learning with others. I've even done a pretty good job of investing in others. But what I haven't done the best, and what I am currently working hard on, is giving myself away up close and personal to others. What I am learning along the way is that doing this is affecting me as much as it affecting the people I'm trying to impact. I think in some ways I always knew this. But too often I tried to avoid it.

Cups, Strainers and Pitchers

To put this in a metaphor that may help us see what I'm talking about, let's think about three items that can be found in any kitchen. The first is a cup. The job of a cup is pretty simple. It holds whatever is put into it. Good cups hold the liquid securely. Bigger cups hold more than smaller cups. Sippy cups have different features than thermoses. But at the end of the day, all cups have one thing in common — they hold liquid.

Strainers are just the opposite of cups. Because they have so many holes, liquid flows out of them. In fact that is exactly what they are built to do. Most of the time strainers are used to remove the liquid from something. Every time we cook pasta, we use a strainer to get the liquid out. As with cups, there are all kinds of strainers. There are big ones and little ones. There are plastic ones and metal ones. But at the end of the day all strainers have one thing in common: they have holes that let the water out as quickly as possible.

Most ideas of discipleship and mission fit one of these two types of kitchen utensils. Often discipleship is described like the cup. The goal of discipleship often becomes holding more and more, and the best disciple is the one who holds the most stuff. So we work to graduate from sippy cups to 32-ouncers and finally to supersized thermoses. The problem is that describing spiritual growth like a cup is that it too often looks more like addiction than addition. In other words, like a junkie we live for a bigger and bigger fix and we require more and more to feel full, but we rarely affect anyone else.

The opposite of the cup is the strainer. The strainer prides itself on its porous features. Every bit of liquid that is poured into the strainer comes out. And it comes out immediately. Liquid passes through the strainer but it doesn't stay in it. Nothing is left to marinate. Lots of missional lives look a lot like a strainer, especially in the generation that is coming up today. We pride ourselves on causes and social action. We want to be used. But we rarely have any time to let anything marinate. So while a lot of good stuff passes through our lives (and that's good), often we are left with too little to be truly satisfied. In the name of service, we are left with little substance.

There is a better way to do life. It's a way that incorporates both the act of holding and the act of giving. This way can best be illustrated in a pitcher. A pitcher is designed to hold what is poured into it. And it is also designed to release what has been placed in it. The good news about the pitcher is that it can hold liquid for a substantial length of time. But to fully accomplish its purpose it must do more than hold liquid. It must pour liquid out. The same is true, I think, of the discipleship process. Part of discipleship is mission. Mission is more then missions. It is more than a project or a place to go. Mission is pouring your life into the life of someone else.

this can be
a individual or corporately

Not Two but One

I think part of what is wrong with our present understanding of making disciples in America today is our continued insistence on separating discipleship from evangelism and mission. You hear it in our language. You see it in the way we staff our churches. You sense it in our understanding of the gospel. And mostly you see it because too many of us don't do either.

Maybe discipleship and mission were never meant to be separated. Maybe they are one and the same. Maybe part of becoming a disciple is being an evangelist. And maybe part of doing evangelism is inviting people to become a disciple. This is the biggest difference between the Christianity of conversion and something more substantial to which I think Jesus was pointing.

We all are supposed to be able to hold something substantial. God wants to indwell us. He wants us to know him and sense him in a deep and meaningful way. But each of us was also created with a spout. The things God places in us are not meant to be held only by us. We are to pass them on. And as we pass on the things that have worked deeply in us, we begin to accomplish the purpose for which we were created. If we fail to pass on the stuff we learn, not only do we fail to affect those around us; we also cease to become what we were created to be. In the end we become something less than who Jesus would be if he were us.

Who we are created to be

Do What I Do

This might be why Jesus was so insistent on his disciples taking part in his ministry while he was here. Sure, he could have done it better than them. But part of Jesus' discipleship training was sending the disciples out to begin making disciples. Just before Jesus fed the five thousand in Mark 6, Jesus sent his disciples out to do the kinds of things he has been doing for them and for others. "Then Jesus went around teaching from village to village. Calling the Twelve to him, he began to send them out two by two and gave them authority over impure spirits. These were his instructions: 'Take nothing for the journey except a staff — no bread, no bag, no money in your belts. Wear sandals but not an extra shirt. Whenever you enter a house, stay there until you leave that town. And if any place will not welcome you or listen to you, leave that place and shake the dust off your feet as a testimony against them.' They went out and preached that people should repent. They drove out many demons and anointed many sick people with oil and healed them." (Mark 6:6-13)

This may also be why Jesus continued to invite them in when 5,000 men plus women and children needed something to eat because Jesus had preached too long at the evening service. Jesus' challenge to Philip seems stark to us: "You give them something to eat."[16] What was Jesus doing? I think he was letting Philip know that he was designed to be a pitcher and not a cup. Jesus was teaching Philip that he was designed to be part of the mission and that being a disciple meant being missional. Mission and evangelism were more than the outcome of the discipleship process; they were part of the discipleship process.

Getting Better

While I told you that this is the part of the discipleship process that I have struggled with most, it doesn't mean I haven't done it at all or that I am not trying to get better at it. As I write this chapter, I think about how there are lots of people who have been impacted by things that I have allowed God to pour out of my life. I won't list their names here, but I continue to stay in contact with many of these

---

[16] This story is found in Matthew 14, Mark 6, and Luke 9.

people as I hope to pass on to them a little of what has been passed on to me.

Still, I have lots of room for improvement. And my hunch is that maybe you do too. As with everything that I have shared so far, there is part that I have embraced. There is part that I am embracing. And there will always be more that I need to and will embrace. I haven't arrived, and neither have you. But I am getting better, and so can you.

Jesus asked the man at the pool of Bethesda, "Do you want to get well?" (John 5:6) I hear that same question in my ear in my places of paralysis. I've sat by the pool and watched it become stirred. I've seen others make it in. But now, as I sense Jesus walking toward me, I hear him asking me that haunting question. And deep inside I know I do want to get well.

I hope I always do. I hope I never get sick of hearing him ask me. And I hope for many more moments of walking and leaping and praising God in the process. I know that this is just my present area of weakness. It may not be presently be yours. But whatever your weakness is, whether it's something we have already discussed, what we are discussing now, something we will discuss, or something that's not even addressed in this book, why not take a moment to hear him speak? And why not let him heal you? It's the way movement is created.

Finding Someone to Disciple

If healthy disciples are people who are becoming disciples partly by helping other people become disciples, then who is around your life that you can help? Who are you letting in to your life? Who might want in on your life? And who might look like Christ more because you did?

The truth is that there is at least one person. If making a disciple is part of becoming a disciple, then someone has to be a part of your life in order for you to give your life away. And my belief is that this person is actually already there. We just need to open our eyes. I can't tell you how many people I have come across who would love someone to invest in them. Somehow, they have grown up in communities and schools and churches without this kind of mentoring touch. Now, they are looking for it yet still can't seem to find it.

Part of solving this problem is making sure the looking is going both ways. We need to respond to people who are wanting someone to disciple them with people looking to make disciples. Sometimes these people will present themselves to you, and all you need to do is really open your ears. At other times you might see someone who has lots of potential or is in a situation in life that you once found yourself in, and so you go to approach that person and offer your help, life, and expertise.

The looking and seeing and finding comes from each perspective and collides together in healthy discipleship communities. *The lack of this kind of looking and seeing and finding results in one group going under-formed and the other group looking deformed.*

Who Needs Who
As you give yourself away to others, you also will find that you are receiving as much if not more than you are giving. It's amazing the grace that is available in the kingdom life. What looks like a waste of time is often the best use of our time. In the end, the one we are helping is not the only one getting help. The one we are discipling is not the only one being discipled. Rather, as we give ourselves away, we position ourselves to receive more from God.

The Bible is filled with stories and parables of this kind of grace. When we put our five talents to work, we get grace for five more. When we use the last of the oil and flour to bake our last cake, we miraculously find the oil jar refilled. In other words, in the kingdom we don't always receive more just by asking for it. We receive more when we are giving more. We become refilled when we are poured out.

So we need others to invest in, as much as they need us to invest in them. It's a two-way street. We help them meet and embrace God. And as we help them do this, God meets and embraces us. There is simply nothing more powerful in the discipleship process than the transference of Spirit birthed in revelation from one life to another.

Information and Imitation

Remember, this transference is not just a transmission of information. It is more than preaching or teaching a Sunday school class. Of course, it may include these things, but it has to be more than these things. This is because discipleship is more than information. It is imitation. And imitation means letting someone come into your life and walk beside you enough to mirror you.

It means inviting someone past the periphery and into the priority. It means inviting someone past the happenstance and into the house. *It's more than accidental relationship. It's intentional access.* And through this intentional access, you give someone the opportunity to stand beside your shoulder and learn what you have learned from others. Then you place that person on your shoulders and help him or her accomplish more than you have. In this process both of you end up looking more like Jesus.

I recently read a Facebook post that quoted a representative of Compassion International from East India. He said, "If you want to run fast, run alone. If you want to run long, run with someone." Taking time to help those behind you may seem like an inefficient waste of time. It may feel like it is slowing you down. But in the end, the movement runs both longer and faster because you ran with someone.

Redefining Normal

As I told you earlier, when I played soccer in college, my coach challenged me and my teammates to coach others in the offseason. He knew that by coaching others, we would pick up more of what he was teaching us and become better players in the process. Never was this more true for me than the year I tore the anterior cruciate ligament in my knee and spent more time than I expected on the sidelines.

During this time I learned more than I ever could have imagined. Because I was still training others, I was still playing. I was still improving. I was still becoming.

Just as I became a better soccer player by coaching others, God has invited us to become more like Him by helping others be like him. When we pass him on to others, we look more like God. That is because perhaps the best Pitcher of all is God himself. In his kingdom the way up is the way down. He is the most unselfish being in the entire universe. He consistently pours himself into us. And he invites us to do the same for others.

Some of you have been pouring for a long time. If this is you, right now where God needs to work on you is in the holding. Your straining has left you strained. So the invitation for you is to marinate a while. Let what God is doing in you remain in you.

But some of you have been marinating for far too long. In this chapter you've realized that you are made to be much more than a cup. You are meant to be a pitcher. So why not let God take you by the handle and pour you out for a moment? It may feel like you are being emptied, but in a really weird way you might also feel like for the first time you are also truly full.

CHAPTER
TWELVE

Skeleton Bones

"The great Christian revolutions come not by the discovery of that which was not known before. They happen when someone believes radically that which has always been there."
— H Richard Niebuhr

"Can these bones live?" —
—*Ezekiel 37:3*

*C*hurch is not a building. It's not a program. It's not even a worship service. Church is supposed to be a people movement. It's supposed to be a group of people gathering in all kinds of different ways to take on Christ's way of life and pass it on to others. It's a place where we find someone to learn from, someone to learn with, and someone to teach. It's a place of discovery and discipleship. It's a place of ministry and mission. It's a place where Christ's presence is manifested in Christ's people.

Unfortunately, this is not what many people they think of when they think of church. For lots of people, the church represents just another business or institution trying to take up their time or take away their money. It represents a place of dogma, not discovery. It represents manipulation, not ministry. So people avoid church more than they approach it. They stay away more than they stay around. And while this truth used to be recognized only in secret, today the secret is out.

In generations of the recent past, we may have been able to position church as buildings and programs and services. Today we cannot. The most recent numbers suggest that just 4 percent of the millennial generation is coming back to church.[17] Better buildings, better programs, and better worship services will not solve this problem, at least for most places. So what will?

Breath. Wind. Spirit. God blowing through and creating a God-dreamed community that is redefining normal.

Ropeless Jump Ropes
The birth of a new millennium has brought with it the birth of many new things. Things like the internet, the smart phone, and the flat-screen television were

---

[17] I first heard this statistic from our partners at 3DM

futuristic novelties at the beginning of the 1990s. Now in 2011, these things are everyday necessities. Those of us who were alive before these things were invented don't know how we ever lived without them. Besides inventions, one of these everyday developments in the new world is what we know as reality TV.

On reality TV, everyday activities and hobbies such as living with roommates, cooking, singing, and working are not scenes in television shows; they actually become the television shows. Shows like *American Idol*, *The Real World*, *Survivor* and *The Biggest Loser* dominate the TV schedule, and all of America is watching.

One reality TV show that popped up (and quickly disappeared) at the beginning of the reality TV revolution was a show called *American Inventor*. On this show, would-be inventors brought their best inventions to a panel of judges in order to see if what they had invented might actually be the next revolution. The winner of the competition was going to win a million dollars worth of business support, entrepreneurial counsel, physical resources, and prize money.

We watched as people brought in inventions and presented them to the panel. Some of these inventions were ridiculous. When we saw them, we laughed at the thought of someone sacrificing their life for the belief that what they invented could actually change the world. On the other hand, some of the inventions were fantastic. When we saw them, we kicked ourselves for not thinking of the invention first.

At about the same time this show hit the airwaves, I read an article about a man who had come up with an invention that was catching a lot of people's attention. He wasn't on the *American Inventor* show, but he should have been. His invention was the Ropeless Jump Rope. He billed it as a jump rope for clumsy people or as exercise equipment for places like prison where a rope could be used for things far less beneficial than exercise. The key to the Ropeless Jump Rope was the weighted handles, which made it feel like you were jumping rope even though there was no rope.

As I read about his invention, I was surprised that the inventor had actually received a patent for his device. After all, the invention just seems odd. When I read the article, the inventor was still working on the prototype. Later, I saw the final product advertised in an airplane magazine where lots of these kinds of things are advertised. I'm not sure anyone ever buys anything from an airplane magazine, but lots of things are advertised in them.

As I read the article, I thought to myself that this prototype wouldn't be hard to produce. So, I went to Walmart, bought a jump rope, and cut the rope off of both handles. I had created my own ropeless jump rope! I jumped and twirled the handles like I was jumping an imaginary rope. The good news is that I found that I could do all kinds of tricks with a ropeless jump rope that I could never do with a real jump rope. I could double jump. I could turn sideways. I could crossover. I could walk the dog. (I'm pretty sure that's a yo-yo trick, but I could still do it.)

The only problem was that as I jumped, I found that I didn't have to jump very long before it began to feel like something was missing. I mean really, didn't this entrepreneur just invent jumping while twirling little sticks? When I used my homemade prototype, I was jumping, but I wasn't really jumping rope. How could I be if the rope was missing?

I bring up this picture because I think a similar thing is going on with church today. We can do all kinds of tricks. We build bigger buildings. We plan better programs. We produce better services. It feels good at first. But it's only a matter of time until we too feel as if something is missing. And that is because something is. Too often we have traded the organic, life-giving power of the Spirit for lights or facilities or personalities. We have church, but the church is missing. A.W. Tozer writes "If God decided to take the Holy Spirit out of the world, the church wouldn't know the difference and would continue to do the same thing." Sad, but true.

Now this doesn't mean that I'm against buildings and programs and programmed services. Remember, overreaction is almost always worse than the original mistake. But I do believe that church is supposed to be something more than buildings and programs and programmed services. And I believe it is the most important job for disciples in our time to find out what is missing and get it back.

Bones

The good news is that we are not the first group of God followers to face this kind of reality. Long before the millennial generation started leaving the church without returning, the prophet Ezekiel faced a similar crisis. God's people, the nation of Israel, had abandoned God, and God had returned the favor by withdrawing His presence from the temple. That left the people alone, vulnerable, and unprotected. The problem was that most of the people of Ezekiel's day didn't even know that He was gone — at least for a while.

What followed was one of the darkest moments in Israel's history. The empire of Babylon invaded the Israelites' land, destroyed their most sacred places, and carried off their most prized possessions as well as their sons and daughters. A trail of blood and humiliation flowed from the temple toward Babylonian territory. It looked as though the nation of Israel had suffered a fatal blow. The people of God were dead. They were scattered. They were dry.

During this devastating reality, God spoke to a prophet named Ezekiel through a vision. In this vision, God brought Ezekiel to a valley where the bones of Israel were scattered across the ground. These were not just any bones. They were the bones of Ezekiel's people — his family, his friends, his nation. As Ezekiel, surveyed the situation, God came to Ezekiel with a penetrating question: "Can these bones live?" (Ezekiel 37:3)

I love Ezekiel's answer. He said, "Sovereign LORD you alone know." This is a biblical way of saying, "I don't know. They are really, really dead God. They are way past CPR. I've surveyed the scene and it doesn't look good, God."

I love Ezekiel's answer because it is so honest and real. He didn't diminish the people's pain by giving a Sunday School answer about God's power. He didn't diminish God by giving a cynical answer or one that only took into account what he could see. He said he didn't know. And in this "I don't know" moment, God began to do some of his greatest work. The work began when God asked Ezekiel to start speaking. The speaking of the Word brought together the bones and then the ligaments and then the flesh. Suddenly, what was a bunch of bones began to look more like a group of people.

Still, there was no life. So God told Ezekiel to speak to the wind. In the Hebrew, wind and breath and Spirit are the same word. As Ezekiel spoke to the wind, the wind of the Spirit gave birth to breath, and like the scene in Genesis 2, the breath once again gave life. What started out as a graveyard had become a vast army.

This was a deeply moving and inspiring vision for Israel, and I think it can be just as inspiring for every follower of God who has surveyed God's people and wondered if they could live again. The ancient/future collision of Word and Spirit produces what temples or buildings, rituals or programs, and sacrifices or services could never do on their own. And this collision mobilizes the followers of God.

Gaining Mobility

Today the people of God once again need to gain their mobility. Graveyards need to be spoken into. The people of God need to be called forth. The Spirit of God must blow in again to give life where it seems only dead things remain. Vision must give birth to word. Word must give way to Spirit. And Spirit then can give opportunity for breath and life and movement.

This is what the church should be and do. It is a people movement brought together by Word and Spirit, gathered by vision and reality, and readied to battle for what should be in the world. It is violent, but not in the way the world is violent. It's violent in the way that true love is violent. It fervently overwhelms with grace instead of furiously overpowering us with guns. It is community pressed by passion. It is community moved by mission. It is community driven by discipleship. And so it is community that looks more like an entity and less like an institution.

This community is not a new invention. Instead, it is the reclaiming of an old one. It is revolutionary in the way that most great Christian revolutions are.

H. Richard Niebuhr states it this way: "The great Christian revolutions come not by the discovery of that which was not known before. They happen when someone believes radically that which has always been there."

Becoming an Army

Understanding church as an entity and not an institution frees us to think differently in how church might function. Church is anywhere that people gather to become more like Christ and to pass on the way of Christ to others. It is not dependent on a building or a program or a service. It is not tied to a tithe or attendance.

Again, this does not mean that buildings and programs and services and tithes and attendances are not useful. *It just means they aren't foundational.* Just as an army is resourced by a base but rarely battles on that base, the church is a force on the offensive in the world, a force taking ground for the kingdom of love in grace. Services and building and programs may resource the movement, but they are not the movement. The movement is what happens when we all seek after Christ by living our lives side by side with someone to learn from, someone to learn with, and someone to teach. It is a movement powered by life lived in imitation of those who help us look more like Christ. And this happens not just on Sunday but every day.

Let me take a minute to return to our Equation of Resemblance and suggest how this might work.

$$\frac{\text{The life Jesus lived}}{\text{Who Jesus was}} = \frac{\text{X (The life I should live)}}{\text{Who I am}}$$

Remember, we are trying to form our lives off of Christ's life. So the way that Christ lived over who Christ was should determine the way I live over who I am. Christ is the basis of the pattern. But watching others helps me see how the resemblance can emerge in different personalities, giftings, and limitations. As I see others become like Christ, I have something to imitate in my life.

This also works in reverse. As others in the world see our lives, they begin to see the thing that makes both of our lives make sense. They see Christ when they see Christ forming His life in us.

Representation

This is why the way we battle matters. It's why the way we move makes a difference. I mean this not just in our strategy but as a community. Armies represent kingdoms, and kingdoms represent kings. So how we wage war in many ways determines how others see God. That is why the war we wage cannot be individualistic. We can learn *from* each other, but we must represent God *with* each other. In other words, while your life might help me see part of God's life or my life might help you see part God's life, it will take both of us together to give the world a true picture of who God is. Each of us is called to resemble Christ, but it will take both of us to fill out his shadow. So we battle not on our own and not for our own agendas or initiatives. Rather, we battle together from God's heart, releasing his help by being his hands and feet.

It is in this unity of mind and mission that community is engaged, not *as a single voice, but as a single force in the world.* Together, we are those who look like Christ. And when this happens, something that has been lost in Christianity is regained. No longer an institution or religion, the movement is an entity in relationship, representing a King who wants to release a kingdom that reminds us of how the world should be, of how it was designed to be.

Redefining Normal

Why don't you take a moment to hear the message and join the movement? It is a message of truth colliding with Spirit. It is information and imitation. It is commitment and community. It will help you become more like Christ and will help others see Christ in the church.

Pick someone to learn from.
Select someone to learn with.
Choose someone to teach.
Engage your community — get life from it and give your life to it.

The stakes are too high to play any other way. We need to regain our center. The church must be rebirthed and reformed, and that revolution starts with you and me. John Calvin said not that the church was reformed but that it is constantly reforming. Today we are part of that reformation. Tomorrow we will cheer on those who are reforming our attempts at reform. But somewhere in this continual reformation, the true church is bound to emerge.

And maybe, just maybe, people will begin to like church again, not because they are impressed by our buildings but because they see Christ in His people. All this will happen when the thing that is missing is found and once again allowed to give life in our graveyards. And as it does it redefines normal church.

SECTION
FOUR

The 911

*D*iscipleship is both information and imitation. It is taught and it is caught. It is revelation and it is relationship. I hope that as of now our discussion has demonstrated these ideas. But even this combustible combination of information and imitation does not yet describe fully all that discipleship is. There is still more. While information and imitation lay the rails for what we are supposed to be, imagination is what releases us to actually become what God intended. So discipleship is information and imitation and also imagination. It is taught and caught and also still to be thought. It is revelation and relationship and also a revolution.

I am using the numbers 911 to invite us into this revolutionary call. These numbers stir within us a sense of emergency and awaken us out of our status quo. They call us to mission and require us to adjust. First responders are those who live life for others. They unleash their imagination to defy the status quo and refuse to settle until everything is as it is supposed to be. Yet by living for others, these first responders actually become their greatest selves. Their lives are released from the confines of safety and realized in the midst of desperate need. And often this leads them to dream about how everything might become different.

Discipleship is not just something that changes me. It is something that changes the world through me. Therefore, the ability to dream is inherent to looking like Jesus. It's dreaming not just for self but for the world. It's stepping into the dream and calling it forth as reality. It's releasing the kingdom from my position in covenant with God and others.

One of the most memorable songs of all time was John Lennon's "Imagine". In this song Lennon released a revolutionary call for a kingdom of sorts, and it captured the minds of a generation. While Jesus and Lennon are distinctly different voices, Jesus is no less imaginative. And I think his kingdom is far more compelling. Jesus' understanding and articulation of what could be is even starker than Lennon's call to his generation. And this call from Jesus still lives on and one day will be fulfilled.

At this point, then, we turn our attention from seeing and being to becoming. We move to the right side of the Equation of Resemblance and start to put hands and feet to who Jesus would be if he were us. Who knows what God will release in our world through you? It may cause you to change. But if you are willing to change, we can only begin to dream what will change in the world because you did. The 911 call is ringing. We have reached a state of emergency. It's time for you to become who God always thought you could be. It's time to imagine.

CHAPTER
THIRTEEN

Imitating without Becoming an Imitation

"It is humbling that I cannot be anything I want. I don't get to create myself. I accept myself as God's gift to me and accept becoming that person as God's task set before me."
— John Ortberg

"Very truly I tell you,
whoever believes in me will do
the works I have been doing,
and they will do even greater things than these,
because I am going to the Father."
—John 14:12

*D*iscipleship requires imitating people who look more like Christ than we do. By imitating them, we in turn become more Christ-like. But the goal of discipleship is never to actually become an imitation of someone else. Imitation is a pathway but not a destination. If the pathway becomes the destination, then something will be lost in both the pathway and the destination. The how is never the what, and the what is never the how. Each serves the other.

Imitation helps us look like Christ. But becoming an imitation does not look like Christ at all. Imagination is how I take what I've learned from you so that it becomes complete in me. Imagination personalizes what I've seen modeled in someone else. And so it is imagination that moves me from just looking like the real thing to actually being the real thing.

In other words, discipleship should always include imitation, but it should never become synonymous with becoming generic.

The Imitation

Life is filled with imitations. I know because I've tasted them. I remember vividly as a child when my parents would return from a stewardship conference or come home from a Dave Ramsey class. (OK, it was Larry Burkett at the time.) All kinds of new things would fill our pantries and refrigerators. The budget was under revision, and anywhere my parents could save money was fair game.

Sodas and cereal seemed to be the place where these revisions cut deepest. Dr. Pepper was exchanged for Dr. Thunder. Mr. Pibb became Mr. Pig. Fruit Loops turned into Fruit Spins. Corn Pops gave way to Golden Nuggets of Corn. Lucky Charms became Fortunate Marshmallows. Total was now Almost. No longer did my parents believe the real thing was necessary. They had bought into the lie, and we were their victims.

The lie of the imitation says that you can have all the taste for half of the cost. "No need to go with the brand name," the imitators say. "Our product looks the same. We just chose to forego four colors on our boxes and saved you what we saved on marketing." The only problem with this idea was that it wasn't the same product.

My mom and dad spent lots of time trying to convince us that there was no difference between the imitation and the real thing. But we kids knew that there was. Maybe not at first, but soon we knew. The imitation often tastes like the real thing at first. It's not until the aftertaste that you realize you have been duped.

Unfortunately, what we also found out about the imitation was that if we ate or drank it long enough, we could convince ourselves that it was just like the real thing. But that only lasted until we went to one of our friend's houses where they had the real thing. In that moment when we tasted the real thing, we once again realized just how much Fortunate Marshmallows fell short in comparison to Lucky Charms. The imitation simply could not compete with the original.

I bring that up to tell you that becoming something less than the real you is exactly the opposite of what discipleship is all about. Discipleship is never about the real thing creating little generic things that look and taste real at first but in the end never quite live up to what's real. Discipleship isn't even about becoming a generic version of Jesus. Let me say this clearly: It is never OK to become a generic of anyone or anything in the name of Jesus. And any discipleship method that doesn't help you become the real you is something less than the movement that Jesus gave his life to create. It may cost less to become someone else, but it will leave an aftertaste both in your life and in the lives of everyone to whom you want to minister.

As a discipler, my goal is not to make you a ripped-off version of me. Rather, it's to turn you into the real you. It is to instill in you the substance that all real things are made of and then give you freedom to express Jesus inside your personality, giftings, callings, and limitations. It's not about you becoming me or me becoming you. It is about each of us becoming who Jesus would be if he were us.

This requires lots of hard work. It includes information and imitation. The information helps me discover and process who Jesus is. The imitation helps me see Jesus' life worked out in others. But it is only as I engage my imagination that I can begin to see who I might be if Jesus were me. This means understanding who I am, who I could be, and then how I might live.

Greater Things

The good news is that this engagement of our imagination is part of exactly the kind of movement that Jesus came to release in the world. Jesus wasn't hoping that his disciples would be lesser versions of himself or that we would live life with painted faces. He wasn't trying to make clones or clowns. In fact, his hopes were quite the opposite.

In John 14, Jesus was sitting in some of his final moments with his disciples. He had broken bread and instituted a new covenant with them. He had shared his life with them. He knew in these moments that his time with them was coming to a close. So he looked again at this motley group of men who had learned to imitate his life, and he inspired them with these words, "The words I say to you I do not speak on my own authority. Rather, it is the Father, living in me, who is doing his work. Believe me when I say that I am in the Father and the Father is in me; or at least believe on the evidence of the works themselves. Very truly I tell you, whoever believes in me will do the works I have been doing, and they will do even greater things than these, because I am going to the Father." (John 14:10-12)

These words are astounding if you think about it.

Something more than imitation is going on. Imagination is now coming into play. How could the disciples do greater things than Jesus? How could the servant actually become greater than the master? It happens because the master gives his life to make it happen.

The best news is not that Jesus said these words. It is that these words actually happened. The disciples did do greater things than Jesus. It seems kind of weird to say, but it's true. The rest of the New Testament itself gives testimony to it.

Maybe it was because Jesus didn't have Jesus to invest in him like the disciples did. Or maybe it was because the kingdom often works upside-down to the way we normally engage the world. Either way, by making his disciples greater, Jesus shows us that true discipleship looks like making people better than ourselves.

None of these disciples looked exactly the same. None of them were carbon copies or ripped-off generic versions of Jesus. But each of them carried Jesus' DNA in their lives. They resembled Christ in their actions. And the world was flipped upside down because they did.

Making it Personal

I believe that Jesus is still speaking the same words he spoke to his disciples two thousand years ago to you and me right now. You were never meant to become a generic version of your pastor or your youth minister or your mentor. You are supposed to become the real you. Not any you that you want to be, but the real you that God first imagined you to be. God doesn't measure you by your performance, but he calls you to be productive in a way that can only happen when you embrace your identity. And to see this identity, you will have to engage your own imagination.

This journey comes with both giftings and limitations. It happens not through self-aggrandizement (thinking more of yourself) or self-determination (trying to make more of yourself) but through the understanding of our true identity. It means both good things and bad things to our hopes and aspirations. It's not about just having any dream you want for your life. Rather, it's about realizing God's dream with who you are. I love the way that John Ortberg describes this: "It is humbling that I cannot be anything I want. I don't get to create myself. I accept myself as God's gift to me and accept becoming that person as God's task set before me."[18]

Using your imagination is first learning to see yourself the way God sees you.

---

[18] John Ortberg, *The Me I Want to Be* (Grand Rapids, Mich., Zondervan, 2010) 17.

This happens initially by coming to a deep understanding that as followers of Christ, we are God's sons and daughters, made to represent him in all we do. And we are Jesus' brothers and sisters, co-heirs with Christ to all God has. But it also goes further and suggests that each of us has a unique person to become in our Father's house and a unique role to play in the family business.

Different by Design

Embracing your identity and living out this identity is part of God's plan. If God had wanted us all to be the same, then he would have created us that way. But we aren't the same. Not even our thumbprints are exactly like. So maybe our desire for uniqueness is born in the heart of God himself. But uniqueness should never be confused with independence. We are created to be unique. As we talked about earlier, we are masterpieces not machines. But we were never meant to live solely on our own. Our lives are derived from Christ's life. His imagination births our imagination. So we walk our road of uniqueness dependent on both God and each other as we imagine who each of us might become to best resemble Jesus.

Part of this discovery comes not just through the discipline of theology but also through the disciplines of psychology and sociology. Discovering who you are and where you live is part of discovering who God has created you to be. And discovering who you have been created to be helps you better understand the Creator himself. Therefore, psychology and sociology should never be seen apart from theology, but instead as smaller parts of the whole.

There are many personality studies and assessments that can help us learn more about who each of us is as a person. Multiple sociological studies can help us learn more about who our community is as a people. We should engage all of this as we seek to become more like Christ. One caveat: as we learn about ourselves and the context of the community in which we live, we must keep in mind that these things are never excuses to avoid change and stay who we are. Instead, they should be inspirations and hints of who we might become.

Identity, Intimacy and Integrity

As we seek to embrace the uniqueness God has given us, one of the most important spiritual roads we can travel down is the road of identity, intimacy and integrity. This is the road on which we become the real us.

Identity refers to who God has created us to be. We are made in his image and made to be his representatives in the world. As those handcrafted in the womb, we demonstrate the creativity of the Creator by embracing our uniqueness.

Intimacy refers to the relationship in which we receive our identity from God. We do not find our identity from within. It comes from God our Father. It is inspired by and available to us through Jesus our Brother. And it is sealed and completed in us by the Holy Spirit who is our guide and companion.

Integrity refers to the authentic expression of our identity in life. It is about being true to who God has imagined and inspired us to be. It authenticates the real us in real life. Living out anything other than who we are created to be is a form of sin.

This explains why sin is so destructive to humanity. Sin is more than disobedience; it is what happens when the real us is replaced by a generic imposter. We break God's heart when we do it, and we also break ourselves and betray our identity in the process.

Identity, intimacy, and integrity are pursuits worthy of our entire lives. Knowing more about who we are, about whose we are, and about how we can be who we are should be lifelong pursuits. As we grow in these areas, we also grow in our imagination of who God is calling us to be. And as we grow in this imagination, we begin to look more like who Jesus would be if he were us.

This is one of Jesus' greatest gifts to us. He died on the cross to make it possible for us to live with our identity, intimacy, and integrity intact. He also showed us a picture of what life might look if identity were not in crisis, if intimacy were not in rupture, and if integrity were not in question. From his life of completeness, we find inspiration for our lives to come into completion.

Character and Competency

Now let's depict the opportunity and challenge that identity, intimacy, and integrity set before us. We'll do this by charting character and competency. Character and competency are the outgrowths of this dynamic identity, because they demonstrate to the world whom God has made and is making us to be. Deficiencies in our character and our competency keep us from becoming all that we were meant to be and keep us from impacting the world around us in demonstrable ways.

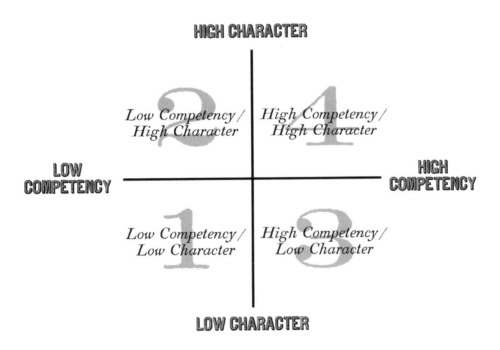

Here are some possibilities for life on the graph that we have created:

Low Character/Low Competency: (Quadrant 1) If you have low character and low competency, you will not accomplish anything good, but you will not affect too many people because of your lack of competency.

Low Competency/High Character: (Quadrant 2) If you have high character but low competency, there is a limit to the good you can create.

High Competency/Low Character: (Quadrant 3) If you have high competency but low character, there is no limit to the harm you can cause.

High Competency/High Character: (Quadrant 4) If you have high competency and high character, you are unlimited in the good God can create in you, and so you can create unlimited good as you change the world.

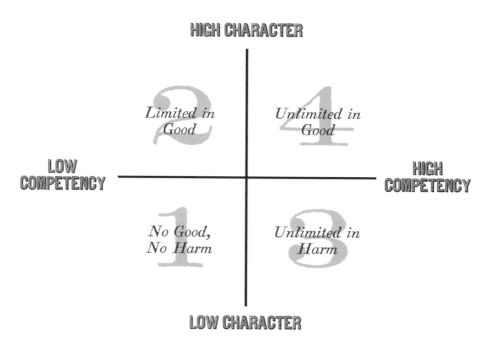

HIGH CHARACTER

Limited in Good — 2

Unlimited in Good — 4

LOW COMPETENCY

HIGH COMPETENCY

No Good, No Harm — 1

Unlimited in Harm — 3

LOW CHARACTER

The truths we see on this graph are the challenges and opportunities of our real lives. We must work toward having both character and competency in order to be an unlimited force of goodness in the world. One is not enough. Sadly, most places in the world will not pay you to work on your character, but they will blame you when your character does not hold the weight of your skill. Christians today err on both sides. We seem to value one or the other but not both. All of us, however, have seen what happens when only one or the other is demonstrated. And one without the other is never good.

Redefining Normal

As we review the Equation of Resemblance once again, we must remember that knowing who Jesus is and the life Jesus lived is only part of the discovery process. Learning about ourselves is necessary, and it is a way we honor God. By observing all the little intricacies of who God has created us to be, we can best begin to see how each of us can uniquely look like Jesus.

But the discovery of self is not the same as humanism or self-help. Both of those ideas are only cheap imitations of the real thing. Rather, the discovery of self is the journey of finding our identity through intimacy and living out that identity with integrity. The discovery of self plays out in both our character and our competency. Most of all, it is about becoming the real us that God had in mind from the beginning.

We simply cannot become who we were created to be without naturally looking more like Jesus. There may need to be some muck and mire scraped away from the canvas of our flesh along the way. But like any good creation, we glorify the Creator best when what he imagined is truly on display in our lives. This will never be generic. It will never be an imitation. It will be the real thing. So stop settling for anything less than the real you. Engage your imagination and savor the taste of the real thing.

CHAPTER
FOURTEEN

Life without Walls

"I do not pray for success. I ask for faithfulness."
— Mother Teresa

"Filled with compassion,
Jesus touched him."
—Mark 1:40-42

*W*e do not discover nor do we live out identity, intimacy and integrity in a bubble. They are pursuits that happen in the midst of everyday life. They do not come to us outside our world; they happen inside of it.

This begs the question, then, of what the Christian posture toward the world should be. I believe this question is one of the most important questions of our day. Many Christians have answered this question in diverse ways throughout our Christian past. H. Richard Niebuhr's brilliant book *Christ and Culture* articulates at length the variety of Christian responses to the world. Niebuhr tells how Christ against culture, Christ for culture, and Christ in the midst of culture are just a few of the postures that well-meaning Christians have taken to describe as Christ's stance in regard to the world. We need only to take a glance around to find entire churches and denominations devoted to one of these stances or another.

In this chapter, I don't intend to endorse one of these articulations but instead to again push us out of our two-dimensional interpretations of Jesus' life toward a three-dimensional understanding. As Niebuhr points out, the truth is that Christ engaged culture in many different ways. Sometimes he stood against it. Sometimes he stood with in it. Sometimes he endorsed it. Sometimes he refused to be enslaved to its understandings. But everything he did engaged it in some way.

Jesus did not live walled off from his world. He was dynamically engaged with and in it. And he engaged his world with a sense of imagination that refused to settle for the status quo or to believe that the commonly made choices were the only options available. Because he engaged his world, the world changed. But this happened with real intrusion mentally, spiritually, emotionally, and physically on his own life. Life without walls came at a cost.

The Day the Walls Came Down
A couple of years ago, my wife and I began the long and arduous adventure of

adopting a little boy named Frankie from Haiti. This adoption was birthed from my wife's sense of calling and relationship with the Lord. Soon into the journey, it became part of mine as well. The two-year venture of Frankie coming into our home is one that today I can only describe as a dream come true. It started as an act of imagination, but now it is our everyday reality.

A year and a half into this journey, Kim and I went to visit our son in Haiti to spend some time with him and let him know how much we loved him even before he came to live with us. This entailed a weeklong stay in Port au Prince.

I will never forget the deep and lasting first impression that this tiny little country made on me in that first visit. Haiti is a country marked by both beauty and brokenness. It was this way before the earthquake of 2010. It is that way after the earthquake as well, only now both are easier to see.

I was filled with both excitement and anxiety as we got off the plane and made our way to the missionary house that would be our home for the week. Almost immediately the beauty of the mountain landscape combined with the brokenness of the capital city to stir my inner dialogue and conscience. On this ride from the airport, we were crammed into our host's SUV with more people and luggage than I had ever been crammed in with before. And as we drove crammed in like this, we weaved through a series of roads that had walls on each side.

In Port au Prince, every piece of property is a compound. Fifteen-foot walls with barbed wire on top parallel the roads on both the left and right side. Inside these compounds are houses and yards. And in one particular compound was our son. We spent most of our week inside the compound with Frankie or traveling to another compound to spend some time with other missionaries and people that we knew. But after four days I was getting a little stir crazy, so I asked to take a tour of life outside the walls.

Kim and I loaded into a car with a Haitian national named Junior and drove around the city, hoping to eventually find a city official who could sign a form for our adoption. As anyone who has been to a third-world country knows, travel is an adventure in and of itself. While we rode around with Junior, I noticed the sights and sounds of the market and slums that were becoming evident on both our left and right sides. The walls were still everywhere, only now they were a little smaller and less concrete. I still play that ride back in my mind from time to time.

About midway through this adventure, I began talking with Junior about the United States and asked if he had ever been there before. He said that he had been to Miami a few times. Since I had spent part of my life in South Florida, we talked about Junior's impression of my world. I asked how he liked his visit to the U.S. and what he thought about our life here. Of course, he was very complimentary. But one thing he said stuck out to me. Although Junior loved the States and thoroughly enjoyed each visit, he said a sense of anxiety always accompanied his journey. I wondered why this was the case, and so I asked. His response was one that I will never forget. Junior said, "I don't know how to live without walls."

This was one of those statements that struck me at my core of my being — one that I knew that I would remember for the rest of my life. I played his words over and over in my mind for a while. I have to admit that at first I was pretty proud to be an American and to be from a place where we could live in a society without walls. But then it hit me. It's not that we don't have any walls; it's that most of our walls are invisible. I treasured Junior's words and wrote them down in my creative notebook, where I record such ideas for further reflection and creativity.

Just a few months later, on January 12, 2010, all those walls came down. I remember vividly driving home from Outback Steakhouse with my wife's birthday dinner in tow. Kim called me crying and told me that an earthquake measuring 7.0 on the Richter scale had struck Port au Prince. Thousands were dead. The walls were down. And our son was somewhere in the midst of the chaos.

Thankfully, we found out pretty quickly that Frankie and all the kids from his orphanage were OK after the initial earthquake. But their structures were compromised. For the next two weeks, Frankie slept outside in the yard with everyone else at his orphanage amidst the walls that had tumbled. Immediately the missionaries whom Frankie lived with launched into a whole new level of ministry. Of course we acknowledge that these people we call missionaries were acting heroically long before we started calling them heroes, but when the walls came down their true sacrifice and compassion were evident in astonishing ways. And in a surprise to these missionaries and almost everyone involved, the first night the walls were gone, songs filled the air literally all over the city. The sense of song replaced the security that before only came through walls. Genuine worship emerged.

Two weeks later Frankie came home to live with us. For us his arrival was a little piece of beauty emerging from the brokenness. But even as we embraced our son, we knew that many other stories hung and still hang in the balance.

Life without Walls
I tell this story because I think many of us find ourselves in a similar situation. For much of my life, I was brought up in a Christianity that was defined by its walls. We didn't know how to live without walls. As a result, mission and evangelism were merely strategic initiatives in which we ventured outside the walls for a few moments of engagement with the world. After the initiative was over, we quickly fled back to our isolated compartments of containment to spend the bulk of our lives.

But as I entered college, something happened. The walls fell down. No longer could I follow Christ from the security of the Christian compound and subculture in which I grew up. Well, I guess I could have if I had I wanted to, but something inside of me was pushing for more. I began to sense through both calling and imagination that maybe the Christian life is meant to be lived outside the walls, without the walls. I longed to live life with the walls down. It was dangerous, and I felt vulnerable. But as I did, I found that something more was emerging — genuine worship.

Eventually paranoia gave way to passion. No longer did I want to retreat to life behind walls, because the Jesus I found in the midst of life without walls looked more like the Jesus of the New Testament than the Jesus of my Christian subculture. And my life started looking more like his life in the process. Others began to come to Christ in the midst of this kind of life.

This kind of life, however, did not come without criticism. Some people misunderstood my intention to live like Christ and felt like I was compromising my faith. One of the leaders of campus ministries literally pulled me aside and chastised me for the way I was living. But life without walls was not a compromise of faith for me; it was a demonstration of faith. The only people it didn't make sense to were Christians, which is something I still find kind of amusing. That experience crystallized to me that at some moments in my life, I was going to have to make a choice. Will I follow Christ, or will I try to fit into the bubble of Christianity?

Now 15 years later, I've found other followers of Christ living outside the walls as well. We are starting to re-imagine church in the world rather than outside of it. The process continues to challenge our view of God and Christianity. It's not that I or we have in any way fully arrived, but I have begun to really like the kind of Christians I and we are becoming and the kind of Christian mission I and we see released in the world.

I want to invite you to join us in this kind of life. You were not meant to live behind walls. You were made by God for God to live in this world. It's a world that is filled both with beauty and brokenness. And as you live with the walls down, you too might find that genuine worship can emerge from and with your life.

Getting Permission

The 15 years that I have spent living without walls and inviting others to do the same has basically boiled down to one question: Do we really have permission to live this way? For many this kind of Christianity feels like a compromise of sorts. How can we really be devoted to Christ and engage the dirtiness and brokenness of our world without becoming dirty and broken ourselves?

One story in the New Testament stands as a helpful and compelling commentary on this very subject. It is the story of Jesus' interaction with a man who had leprosy. Jesus had begun articulating his highly imaginative and provocative dream known as the kingdom of God. And the leper wanted to know if the dream was a reality not just for everyone else but for him too. The leper never asked that direct question, but it is housed within his words: "If you are willing you can make me clean" (Mark 1:40) This statement reflected the leper's hope that kingdom could move from Jesus' imagination to his own reality.

I love Jesus' reaction: "Filled with compassion, Jesus reached out his hand and touched the man." (Mark 1:41) The words "filled with compassion" contain within them a sense of sighing in the Greek. It's as if Jesus looked at the man and sighed, signifying that what Jesus saw in the man and his leprosy was not what God intended for us or this world. But with the next few words, all the walls of Jesus' society came crashing down. Jesus reached out and touched him. Jesus sighed when he saw the man, but everyone around Jesus must have gasped when they saw what Jesus did as he placed his hand on the man with leprosy.

In the world where Jesus lived, no one touched someone with leprosy. In fact, drastic measures were taken to make sure that a person with leprosy never came in contact with those who didn't have it. Lepers had to wear torn clothes, stay at least six feet away from anyone else, and yell to those around that they as lepers were "Unclean! Unclean!" so that everyone could make sure to stay away. The reason they did this was because in Jesus' day everyone was working under a certain assumption that when something clean touched something unclean, the unclean thing made the clean thing unclean. (Bet you can't say that last phrase times fast.)

But with Jesus' touch, all the assumptions changed. This time, instead of the unclean thing making the clean thing unclean, exactly the opposite happened. This time, when the clean thing touched the unclean thing, the unclean thing got clean. The man was cured of his leprosy, and the kingdom dream became the kingdom reality. The rest of Jesus' ministry takes on the tone and rhythm of this small story. It's a tone and rhythm that the religious establishment never quite understood. This very act of associating with sinners is what led Christ into his greatest conflict with this religious establishment. Eventually, it led to his crucifixion. But not even this greatest act of evil was unredeemable. Crucifixion turned into justification. All the evil of the world was, is, and will be set straight because through this act the clean is still making the unclean things clean today.

Redefining Faithfulness

In this one act of compassion, Jesus redefined what faithfulness looks like in the kingdom of God. No longer was faithfulness defined by what was not touched. Instead, faithfulness took on an entirely new posture. This moment redefined normal and challenged the status quo. It was more than new wine; it was a new wineskin.

Today our definition of faithfulness is just as much in need of redefinition as in Jesus' day. And so I would like to take a moment to demonstrate exactly what redefined faith might mean for our lives.

Most of the time, when people talk about how to live with God and the world, a few alternatives are given. Each of these alternatives follows the assumed presupposition that we stand between God and the world.

Based on this arrangement, three alternatives are possible. The first alternative is the posture of I call *faithlessness*. In this posture we face the world and turn our back on God. We love the world and hate God. We do our own thing as opposed to God's thing. We seek after the world and walk away from God.

The second alternative is being caught in between God and the world. I call this posture *faltering*. In this posture we have one hand on God and one hand on the world. We want some of God, but we also want some of the world. So we pull on each and are torn between them. It's God on Sunday and the world on Monday. It's God on Wednesday night and the world on Friday night.

The third alternative is the posture of assumed faithfulness. Let's refer to this as *pseudo-faithfulness*, because it's not what I believe real faithfulness looks like. Inside the assumption that we are between God and the world, this posture appears to be the only way we can truly seek God and be sold out for Him. So we turn our back on the world and turn our face toward God. We seek after God with everything we have and leave the world behind.

Christianity spends much time and energy getting people from the first and second alternatives into the third alternative. That's because this pseudo-faithfulness works well at church or at camp. We sing songs and quote verses to state it as our mantra. The only problem is that this posture is impossible to maintain. Sooner or later faithfulness defaults to faltering. We live in the world, and so it is only a matter of time until we feel its tug. So we spend our lives in a dichotomy between Sunday and Monday, and eventually we stop believing that anything other than faltering is really possible.

But maybe there is another way. Just as in Jesus' day, our assumptions need to be challenged. Maybe repentance is not about turning away from the world toward God, but instead going back to the beginning to discover an entirely different posture. Maybe real *faithfulness* looks entirely different. In fact, if we take Jesus' posture in Mark 1 as the norm, then maybe this new posture is actually not just possible but probable. What if, instead of assuming that we stand between God and the world, we gave up the center position to God? What if we got out of the center of our lives and gave God the center?

With this posture, instead of choosing between God and the world, we seek God. And by seeking God, we begin to see the world in a whole new way. As we live in and engage the world through God, the clean thing starts to touch the unclean things. Acts of compassion move in, and the kingdom of God moves from God and our imagination into real life. As that happens, the unclean things get clean. The world changes because God is changing it through us.

Redefining Normal

We cannot solve the Equation of Resemblance in a bubble. It will not happen inside the walls. Jesus engaged his world, and so should we. This is a continuous act that begins in the imagination of God himself. His imagination compels our own. Amazingly, from our imagination, the kingdom of God comes close in our day just as it did in Jesus' day.

So you and I have a role to play. Our opening lines begin with sighs and require a little re-orienting. Eventually sighs give way to gasps as our compassion compels us to touch the unclean. And as we touch the unclean, the miracle of redemption once again comes to view. The kingdom comes, heaven touches earth, and God is on display in us.

This way of life, though, comes at deep personal cost. Life without walls is not always safe. It leverages all of our resources, and it is often questioned by the religious establishment of our day. But the lives of real people hang in the balance. Our quest is not just converting them to our way of thinking about God, but the real possibility that they can actually taste the kingdom of God. And once they taste it, I believe that many of them will want it as their own.

As always, the best part of any good kingdom is the good King that stands in the center of it all. And our King is always good. In fact, his goodness knows no bound. He is still redeeming everything through his cross. Worship emerges as walls are falling down. Heroes are being made. And all this is happening as Christians live lives that are truly faithful.

CHAPTER
FIFTEEN

God's Will and My Life

"People of accomplishment rarely sat back and let things happen
to them. They went out and happened to things."
— Leonardo da Vinci

*"Reaching into his bag and
taking out a stone, he slung it
and struck the Philistine on the forehead.
The stone sank into his forehead,
and he fell facedown on the ground."*
—1 Samuel 17:49

I love Duke University basketball. Few other environments in all of sports compare to the passion and performance that is on display every time a home basketball game is played at Cameron Indoor Stadium in Durham, North Carolina. Because my brother is a grad student there, and has been for quite a long time, every once in a while I get invited to take part in this unbelievable sporting event. And every time I get the chance to go, I am amazed by the culture.

I love Duke basketball because Duke basketball is more than just a good team or a good coach. It's a community on mission, and everyone has a role to play. The Cameron Crazies in the Duke student section camp out sometimes for weeks before games just to get tickets. Coach Mike Krzyzewski is one of the most intense and gifted coaches of all time. Each night he comes out and gives his best and expects his team to do the same. The sold-out gymnasium stands on its feet the entire game. Cheers aren't just for cheerleaders; instead, these chants often start and find strength from within the crowd. And the players almost always give the crowd something to cheer about, as Duke is one of the most successful college basketball programs of all time.

But every time I have gone to Duke to watch a basketball game, one moment has stood out above all the rest. It's a moment that happens at least once every game. The student section starts a cheer calling for Crazy Towel Guy to play his role. Over and over, the student section chants, "Crazy Towel Guy, clap clap, clap clap clap. Crazy Towel Guy, clap clap, clap clap clap." Soon the cheer catches on throughout the entire gymnasium. A minute goes by as the cheer grows louder and louder. Finally, when it feels like the building is about to explode, an older gentleman in the upper center section of the stadium stands up and waves his towel. When he does, 10,000 people go crazy for Crazy Towel Guy.

I love this because to me it's exactly what Duke basketball is really all about. Here is a guy who doesn't have the greatest gifts, talents, or abilities, at least when it comes to basketball. All he does is wave a towel. But somehow he has found a way to attach his small gifts to the big dream of Duke basketball. And as he plays his role, the dream of Duke basketball is realized in greater and fuller capacity.

I think this is a great picture of what life in the kingdom of God is all about. We may not be the most gifted or talented, but all of us can wave a towel. And if we are imaginative enough, maybe we too can find a way to attach our towel-waving selves to God's big dream. In fact, if you listen closely, the cheer is going out for each of us. It's calling us to play our role. It's calling us to be the Crazy Towel Guy or Crazy Towel Girl we always imagined we could be. And as we do, the kingdom is realized by us in our lives and through us in the world.

Waving Your Towel

Each of us has a role to play as God's sons and daughters and representatives in the world. We all have a towel to wave. When we wave it, we resemble Jesus. It starts with a call from God himself. This call catches on through the body of believers known as the church. Finally, it makes its way to us. And just when it feels like the building is about to explode, we stand up and wave it. As we do heaven celebrates.

The towel we wave is our life. When we become who Jesus would be if he were us, we wave this towel. As we do, we solve for X in the Equation of Resemblance, and the life of Jesus lives on in our lives. God's will becomes our way of life, and our way of life manifests God's will.

This journey of aligning God's will and my life is not always easily discovered. Already we have waded through the dense waters of information and imitation to discover the person Jesus is, the life that he lived, and how his life is lived on and passed to others. Already we have begun to realize with our imagination who we are and what our lives might look like if we lived out our identity in the world. But how does this general posture play out in our actual lives? What is the life Jesus would live if he were me? How can I finally solve for X in the Equation of Resemblance?

It will take a keen mind, an aware spirit and a courageous heart to keep moving forward on this journey. But I believe God wants us to find the solution for X as much if not more than we do. Even more, I believe he will help us in the process. To begin this final leg of the journey, I want to turn to one of my favorite stories in all of the Bible. It's a story of a shepherd boy who became the greatest king in Israel's history. I see my story in his story, and we can see your story too.

Shepherd Boy Kings

David is one of the most loved and admired characters not just in the Bible but in all of ancient history. His story tells of a boy who made his way from underdog to overachiever. It's the kind of story that inspires us in the way that all great underdog stories do. It inspires us because it makes us believe that we too can become part of God's great plan.

The story begins in 1 Samuel 16, when David was anointed Israel's future king. David was a curious choice for king. When the prophet Samuel told David's father Jesse that one of his boys was going to be the next ruler of Israel, Jesse prepared a feast and called his boys to line up so that Samuel could make God's choice. But Jesse didn't even think to call in his youngest son, David. Instead, David remained in the shepherd's field tending sheep while his brothers and family tended to Samuel. When Samuel arrived, Jesse presented all of his sons but David to the prophet. First was Eliab, who looked like a king. But he was not God's choice. Then was Abinidab, but neither was he the one for whom God was looking. Next was Shammah, and again the same result. One by one all of Jesse's boys walked by until all had passed. But the king was not yet present.

Finally Samuel asked if Jesse had any more children. Jesse's reply was less than complementary of David. Still, David was summoned from the shepherd's field, and as he stood before Samuel, God made his choice. Samuel anointed David to be king. For David in that moment, a new dream was born.

You would think David's life would be complete at this moment. Actually, though, his life was just beginning.

The unforeseen truth was that there was a long time between the birth of the dream and the dream coming into fruition. David must have wondered in the times between the two if his imagination had played tricks on him. Had he really heard God's voice? Did God really choose him? Or was he making it all up, just trying to find a bit of significance for his insignificant life?

One story within the story makes all the difference. The story of David and Goliath was the defining moment of David's life. In this single moment, David's life turned and launched him in a new trajectory. His life is never the same after this moment. But how did David get to Goliath, much less defeat him? How did this defining moment become reality? And what does this story tell us about how we can learn to recognize our own defining moments when they come into our lives? All these questions will help us as we let David's story inform our own.

The story of David being anointed king gives way to David's story of defeating Goliath in 1 Samuel 17. In between the two stories is David's time in the shepherd's field. The newly anointed king was not whisked away to palace full of people; instead, he returned to a field full of sheep. It would have been easy for David to question God's plan for his life during this time. What did tending sheep have to do with leading people? How could a person as important as him be left with such an unimportant job? But David's response is striking. He didn't complain. He just obeyed. Even when David was left behind as his brothers went off to war, David still trusted God's heart. When Jesse asked David to run a seemingly meaningless errand of bringing cheese and crackers to his brothers on the front lines, David got up early to accomplish his father's bidding.

David's early life is a story of obedience, both obedience to God and to his father. It is a story of trust and a story of training. Back in the mundane moments of the shepherd's field, David obediently learned all that he would need to lead in the future. His brothers were off watching the war, but David was training for battle in ways no one else could see.

David's obedience led him to a place of opportunity. When he brought the cheese and crackers to his brothers, David arrived at the battle to find that no one was fighting. It looked as though history was about to repeat itself. Hundreds of years earlier, on these same hills, spies from the nation of Israel refused to conquer the Promised Land because of the giants they saw. Now one giant was keeping the nation of Israel from God's best all over again. All of Israel quaked in fear of one man who came out day after day and challenged Israel to a mano-a-mano showdown. The problem was that no one other than David saw the opportunity before the Israelites. Everyone else only saw a threat.

When David arrived, he immediately started asking what would be done for the man who defeated this giant. This is an incredibly intriguing moment if you stop to think about it. How did a boy whose life had been confined to tending sheep see more opportunity at the battle line then the men who had been hand-selected for battle? How did David see an opportunity where everyone else saw a threat?

We find out later that it all goes back to those mundane moments in the shepherd's field. David saw what others couldn't because David had been where others hadn't. And back in the shepherd's field, David had seen God deliver him first in small ways and then in bigger ones. Now, as he faced the greatest challenge of his young life, he trusted that God would do the same thing he had always seen God do by delivering him.

All this brings up an interesting thought about trust. You can't know trust. Trust has to be experienced. People who trust God with big things are really people who have learned to trust God with lots of small things. And by learning to trust God, they begin to see the kinds of big things that God might want to do in the world.

Seeing the opportunity, though, was only half of the battle for David. David still had to go on the offensive. David went to Saul, Israel's king at the time, and told him that he would fight Goliath. Saul was skeptical at first, because he didn't really expect much out of David. Still, Saul agreed to let David go out and fight.

To help David, Saul tried to dress David in his royal armor. But the problem was that the king's armor didn't fit David very well. So David, clinging to his own identity and uniqueness, looked back in his life once again, this time to find the weapons with which he would fight. For him, these weapons turned out to be a slingshot and a few stones.

David made his way to the front line and met Goliath. After a little trash-talking on both sides, David and Goliath faced off in what proved to be a short battle. David threw one stone, and it hit Goliath in just the right spot. Goliath fell to the ground, and David cut off his head. The entire Philistine army started to flee, and Israel, which had been cowering in fear, became courageous in battle as it chased the Philistines down and defeated them. And all this happened because David waved his towel. Many more stories follow this defining moment in David's life. Each time, David rose to the occasion.

Simplifying the Sensational

The process that led David from the shepherd's field to the palace is really quite simple. It wasn't a five-year plan or a genius strategy. David simply obeyed God, looked for opportunities, and went on the offensive. In the shepherd's field, David learned who God was. On the frontline he remembered what he had seen God do, both in his life and in Israel's history. And so in the battle, he trusted God to do what he knew God had done again and again and again.

I think the same process can help us as we start to discover and embrace God's will for our own lives. Obeying God is the process of learning all of who God is and following after Him with all that we are. This we have referred to as information. Information comes not in knowledge but in revelation.

Looking for opportunities is allowing what God has done with others to be done in us. It is no coincidence that David was the great-grandson of Ruth and Boaz, nor is it a stretch to think that their story was part of what inspired his story. We have referred to this as imitation. In imitation, revelation becomes relationship.

Then information and imitation led to imagination as David went on the offensive to defeat Goliath. Revelation and relationship find their fulfillment in revolution. The kinsman redeemer in Boaz gives way to the kingdom ruler in David. It's the same big dream, but a different role. In both cases, the towel waves, and heaven celebrates.

Here is how I would draw out the process that we have begun to think about so far:

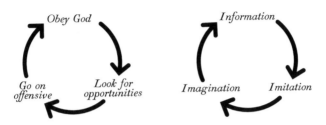

Each cycle correlates and corresponds with the other. Combined together, they work like this:

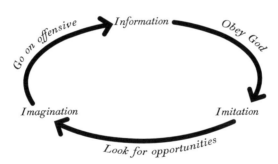

This cycle repeats itself not only in David's life but in my life (and I suspect yours) as well. I learn and I obey. I see in others and I begin to see for myself. I dream for the future and begin to act as if the future is already here and now. And as I do, I create a history of walking with God. Sometimes this looks like success. At other times it looks a lot like failure. But in both my successes and failures, I learn how to live significantly.

I love the way the Leonardo da Vinci described the lives of significant people: "People of accomplishment rarely sat back and let things happen to them. They went out and happened to things." Significance is not about letting things happen. It is about giving your life to happen to things. Significance is David's story, and it can be our story as well.

The X Factor

Once we begin to live our lives in obedience, in opportunity, and on offense, we start to create a history of life with God. As this history becomes more and more substantial, we can actually begin to identify X in our own Equation of Resemblance. Remember, X in our equation is the life that we should live. Here is how that might work.

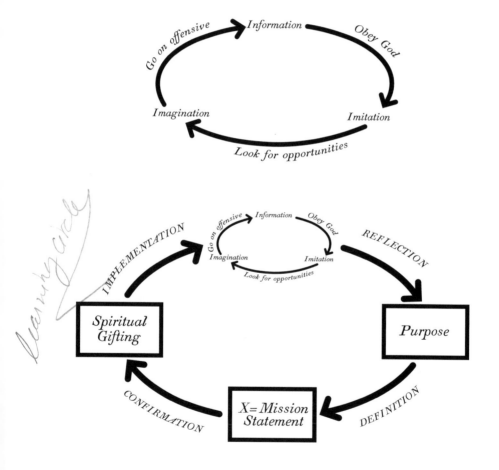

Once we begin to build a history of walking with God in information, imitation, and imagination, we should spend some time in reflection of that history. As we think back about our successes and failures, our growth and maturity, a sense of purpose begins to emerge. We may not be able to articulate it yet, but something begins to stir in our souls. Definition helps us put the stirrings of our soul into words.

Let's get extremely practical now and start to think about how we might talk out God's work in our lives. By developing a mission statement, we begin to articulate what our lives might look like if Jesus were us. Normally, this requires us to work on a definition until we can describe our life in 6-12 words. These words help us state the life we are seeking to live. They are the X in our Equation of Resemblance.

Once we find X we start evaluating and living it out. The process of confirmation and implementation can begin. Confirmation begins with Spiritual gifting. Spiritual gifts never determine our calling; instead, they confirm or caution against what we are beginning to articulate. God will either confirm what we sense is the life that are called to live by equipping us or changing us to complete it, or he will send us back to the drawing board to think more clearly about him and ourselves. Then implementation is the process of actually living this calling out. In the end, the cycle brings us back to information, imitation and imagination.

This circle reminds us that this will be an ongoing process in our lives. As we continue to make strategic time in our year and lives for reflection, definition, confirmation, and implementation, we continue to evolve into who God has called us to be. As we do so, we resemble more and more the pattern and way of Christ. And all of this should take place within a community that speaks into us and helps us perceive, articulate, and evaluate God's work and presence in our lives.

Redefining Normal
Living out God's will for our lives will rarely happen on accident. It won't just happen to us. It will happen with us. And it requires us to play our role in the

process. Obeying God, looking for opportunities, and going on the offensive are the result of discovering who God is, seeing his life lived out in others, and dreaming about what his life might look like in us. As information leads to obedience and imitation leads to opportunity, likewise imagination helps us go on the offensive to make the kingdom dream become our kingdom life.

At any time in this process, God may speak to us and give us through direct revelation what would take process a long time reveal. When this happens, we must do exactly what he says, which leads us back to revelation and obedience.

So, what if you stopped assuming that God wasn't interested in you or that you were too insignificant to be part of his dream? What if I told you that He was calling you in from the shepherd field and anointing you to play your role in his vision for the world? What if you listened close enough to hear the call for Crazy Towel Guy or Crazy Towel Girl and looked down to find a towel in your hand? Would you stand up and wave it? And as you wave it, what would begin to happen not just in you but in our world because you did?

CHAPTER
SIXTEEN

Winning Beautifully

"There is nothing in my life that is not changed
after I have learned to say 'I believe.'"
— Helmut Thielicke

*"Each of you should look not
only to your own interests,
but also to the interests of others."
—Philippians 2:4*

Waving our towel is good. Playing our role in the kingdom of God is significant. Resembling Jesus with our lives is huge. But us finding the solution for X, the life we should live, is not the only goal in the life of the disciple. In other words, we don't wave our towels as a means to finding our own significance. We wave our towels to help the team win.

Far too often the Christian life of one person happens independently of the Christian pursuit of others. We too often seek our own dreams or and try to live out God's will for our lives on our own. We try to become who God has called us to be, but we do so at the expense of keeping others from being who God has called them to be. As a result, the Christian pursuit of significance degenerates and looks a lot like the world's pursuit of success. When it does, the individuality and independence on our "team" creates a losing culture.

How we play our role in the kingdom is just as important as what role we are called to play. How we develop into who God has called us to be is just as important as what God has called us to do. Therefore, our road to faith must look different than the world's journey to fame. We must change in a way that helps change everything.

What Brazil Knows that We Don't
As you may have gathered by now, I am a pretty big sports fan. I grew up playing sports, and along with playing sports, I watch them. For as long as I can remember, I have watched my favorite teams and players play football, basketball, soccer, and golf.

One of my favorite sporting events to watch happens every four years and is called the World Cup. The world basically stops to watch this global competition between countries in the game of soccer (or football or futbol, depending on where in the world you are). This is one of the most watched sporting events of the year, outperforming the Super Bowl, the World Series, the NBA Finals, and any other event the U.S. has to offer. The World Cup is popular because so much national pride hangs in the balance.

In World Cup competition, Brazil has succeeded more than any other country. That's no surprise, because in Brazil, soccer is more than a sport. It is a way of life. Every four years, the World Cup is Brazil's opportunity to demonstrate why it is home to the best soccer in the world.

But Brazil's goal on the soccer pitch is more than winning. The scoreboard determines only half the battle. Truth be told, Brazilians don't only expect their team to win; they assume victory will happen. Because of this assumption, how team Brazil plays is just as important to the country as whether it wins. In Brazil, the goal is to win beautifully. In other words, the style they win with is just as important as the win itself.

Some experts have criticized Brazil for this aim. Some think Brazil would be even more dominant if it weren't as committed to style. And truthfully, the experts are probably right. Playing beautifully has kept Brazil from winning some games that they could have won. But the Brazilians know that when they win beautifully, they change everything. When they win beautifully, the Brazilians don't only bring home a trophy — they leave a legacy.

I think true disciples of Christ understand about life what Brazil understands about soccer. We are playing our role, and we are playing to win. But representing Jesus requires more. We must win beautifully. The style we play with is as important as the outcome we hope to produce. *The way of Jesus is just as important as the work of Jesus.* The goodness we win with is as important as the goodness we create.

As we win beautifully, we not only change our lives; we also play in a way that can change the world. This means going beyond gaining crowns with our life so that our lives have credence and credibility. This does at times increase our chances of losing. But as Christians, we know that even our losing, if done with grace, is really a chance for resurrection to have the final and greatest say.

Playing the Game to Challenge the System

What Brazil knows about soccer, Steve Spurrier knows about football. Steve Spurrier is one of college football's renowned coaches. His dominance in college football has made him a legend at Duke, Florida, and South Carolina. While we know Spurrier as an accomplished coach now, long before Spurrier gained the respect he now has, he coached his teams to play in ways that, if they won, would change the way the game is played. One of these strategies was the innovative spread offense. In this offense Spurrier made unprecedented moves of playing with four or five wide receivers rather than two tight ends or two running backs. Spurrier planned this offense so that it would always have receivers open and therefore challenge opposing defenses with quickness instead of power. When Spurrier introduced this offense at Duke, experts criticized it as a flag-football offense, arguing that while it may have short-term success as people adjusted to it, it would never really be a respectable way to play games.

But something happened that changed everything. Spurrier started to win. He didn't just win; he won big. He didn't just win big; he won in exciting fashion. His teams moved the ball through the air with a beautiful pattern and timing that caught an entire nation by surprise. Before anyone knew what had happened, Spurrier was winning conference championships, and he finally won a national championship. His success didn't just change the culture of Duke and Florida and South Carolina football; it changed the way everyone plays the game. More and more teams started using spread offenses. These offenses changed the way defensive coaches played defense. Today it's harder to find a team that doesn't play with a spread offense in college football than one that does.

Spurrier challenged the system by the way he played the game. When he won, he created a football revolution. Christianity is no less revolutionary. And we too are called to challenge the systems of the world by the way we play the game.

For instance, we should challenge the way business is done by the way we do business. We should challenge the way education is done by the way we do education. We should change the way healthcare is done by the way we do healing. Jesus started these kinds of revolutions in the way he lived his life. His sacrificial submission to the will of the Father cost him his life, but it saved the entire world. The way he laid down his authority changed the political climate of the world. And he did it all not with a sword in his hand but through a secret society that chose to play in a way that changed everything.

Ladders and Elevators

Most of the time, when people talk about success, they use the image of a ladder. We hear this when people talk about climbing the corporate ladder. We refer to climbing the ladder with our possessions when we talk about keeping up with Joneses. And even if we don't refer to it directly with our language, it's the way a lot of us have been taught to think about life.

On the ladder, life is a competition with others. Everyone around us is a potential threat to our success. So to climb the ladder, we pull on the heels of those in front of us and step on the heads of those below us. Because there is only room for one person on each rung, people around us are either stepping stones or obstacles. On the ladder we live our lives for ourselves.

The problem with the ladder is that only one person can be on top of the ladder at a time. As a result it's hard to actually get to the top. And reaching the top is only half of the battle, because staying on top is even harder. So on the ladder, our lives are full of kicking and pulling and pushing everyone around us so that we can maintain or improve our position on the ladder. In the name of success, we break everything that is beautiful in the world, often including the people we love the most.

We all recognize this way of life because we see it every day. Some of us are good at climbing the ladder, and so we are drawn to this system. Others of us reject the system, and so we've stopped trying to ascend altogether. But the answer to ambition gone sour is never a lack of ambition. Passivity is not the corollary of purity. The response to overpowering others is not to deny our power, but rather to use our power to empower others.

I think there is another way to ascend. It's not with a ladder but with an elevator. You don't climb in an elevator; you are raised. And on the elevator, there is room for others to win with you. *Your competition is not with others but for others.* Sometimes you might have to move downward to get others before you ascend to the top. With the elevator, community shares in success, because when one of us rises, we all win. And because we are together, the journey on the elevator is sometimes just as beneficial as the destination.

Becoming who Jesus would be if he were me cannot look the same as becoming who I want to be on my own, only with Christian words. We cannot use a Christian ladder to do it. We must challenge the ladder system altogether by riding in the elevator and inviting others to come along with us. Sometimes this will mean going down before we go up. It may even take longer to get to some floors than if we had chosen to use the stairs. But when we win with the elevator, more people win with us. And as we challenge the system by the way we choose to play the game, the world changes.

Listen to how Paul challenged the Philippian church to resist the ladder and embrace this elevator kind of life:

> Do nothing out of selfish ambition or vain conceit, but in humility consider others better than yourselves. Each of you should not look only to your own interests but also to the interests of the others.
>
> In your relationships with one another, have the same mindset as Christ Jesus:
>
> Who, being in very nature God, did not consider equality with God something to be used to his own advantage; rather, he made himself nothing by taking the very nature of a servant, being made in human likeness. And being found in appearance as a man, he humbled himself by becoming obedient to death — even death on a cross!
>
> Therefore God exalted him to the highest place and gave him the name that is above every name, that at the name of Jesus every knee should bow, in heaven and on earth and under the earth, and every tongue

acknowledge that Jesus Christ is Lord, to the glory of God the Father. (Philippians 2:3-11)

So what does it look like to ride in the elevator? How do we do this with our family, our business, our schools, our churches, our leadership style, and a million other things we could list? It's worth spending our entire lives to go on an adventure to discover such answers. I do not have all of them. But I would like to take a moment to provide a couple of hints on a few.

Winning Beautifully with Our Families

Following Christ and raising a family can be difficult. It is the battle of good loves. So how does our relationship with Christ affect our most central relationships? This battle of priorities is usually answered in one of two ways. Some people neglect their families in the name of Christ. Other people neglect the hard calls of Christ in the name of their families. As you look around the Christian world today, you see byproducts both of these divergent ways of seeing Christ and family.

In the generation before mine, family was too often treated as an obstacle to ladder climbing. Many fathers sacrificed their wives and kids not to spread the gospel but to further their careers. Some misused the gospel as a cover for their own ambitions. It was ladder climbing with a Christian excuse.

I think my generation has made the opposite error. In the name of protecting our families, we have created a system that sounds right at first but ends up in a ditch on the other side of the road. Our generation's error is putting our sense of calling after our sense of family. So we have preached family as our first calling. The mantra is to cheat your call before you cheat your family.

The problem with this perspective is that it is hard to be honest and still align it to the lives of Jesus, Peter, Paul, and just about everyone in the New Testament. Jesus, Peter, Paul, and others had a different perspective. In Mark 3, Jesus' mother and brothers are outside a house where Jesus was teaching. Jesus heard that they are waiting for him outside. Most scholars think they had come to commit him to an insane asylum. When Jesus heard that they were there, he addressed the crowd: "'Who are my mother and my brothers?' he asked. Then he looked at those seated around the circle with him and said, 'Here are my mother and my brothers! Whoever does God's will is my brother and sister and mother.'" (Mark 3:33-35)

In Matthew, Jesus says more shocking words:

> Do not suppose that I have come to bring peace to the earth. I did not come to bring peace, but a sword. For I have come to turn "a man against his father, a daughter against her mother, a daughter-in-law against her mother-in-law — a man's enemies will be the members of his own household." Anyone who loves their father or mother more than me is not worthy of me; anyone who loves their son or daughter more than me is not worthy of me. (Matthew 10:34-37)

Paul encouraged the Corinthians in much the same tone:

> What I mean, brothers and sisters, is that the time is short. From now on those who have wives should live as if they do not; those who mourn, as if they did not; those who are happy, as if they were not; those who buy something, as if it were not theirs to keep; those who use the things of the world, as if not engrossed in them. For this world in its present form is passing away.
>
> I would like you to be free from concern. An unmarried man is concerned about the Lord's affairs — how he can please the Lord. But a married man is concerned about the affairs of this world — how he can please his wife — and his interests are divided. An unmarried woman or virgin is concerned about the Lord's affairs: Her aim is to be devoted to the Lord in both body and spirit. But a married woman is concerned about the affairs of this world — how she can please her husband. I am saying this for your own good, not to restrict you, but that you may live in a right way in undivided devotion to the Lord.
> (1 Corinthians 7:29-35)

What was Jesus saying? Was Jesus encouraging people to neglect their families? Was Paul against the family structure? Personally, I think both Jesus and Paul were advocating something entirely different. Family and mission are not supposed to be in dichotomy with each other. Choosing a priority between the two results from a fallen system of a broken world. Living beautifully means imagining something different. Personally, I think this means developing a family on mission. *The family unit of the New Testament is united not by blood but by mission.* If I am leading my family well, we should all be on this mission together.

This definition of family, then, goes beyond bloodlines. As a father and husband, I should do everything in my power to instill this in my own family dynamic. Creating an extended family means inviting those close in mission into my home. Together we raise our kids, work out our callings, pay our bills, and enjoy the life God gives us. It is not communism, but it is communal. And this creates an atmosphere where family and calling can live together.

Personally, I have seen this work out in my own life in a couple of ways. First, when I was dating, I dated intentionally and had this in mind. I knew that if my relationship with God didn't determine my relationships, then my relationships would soon determine my relationship with God. I had seen too many people sacrifice calling in the name of love, and so I determined to find someone who would work out the call of Christ with me instead of holding this call against me.

Second, Kim and I make a concerted effort to not talk of my work as work. We use words like calling and mission in our family. So when I travel to speak, or when our sense of calling asks us to do hard things, it is not because of dad's ambition to climb a ladder but because of God's call on our family. We also encourage all of our family to be part of the mission. *It is not my calling. It is our calling, and each of us has a role to play — a towel to wave. Mission is the family business.*

The extended family network was the dynamic that changed the world. It was a family on a mission. Some of this family was blood, and some of it was not. But this group of people acted as a family that was united by mission.

In case you are wondering, this is not just a way of life for those of us in professional ministry. It is a way of life for all of us. Our kids need to know that there is more to life than being a successful businessman or a famous actress. The pursuit of money cannot carry the weight of family. But mission can.

Sometimes our jobs are our mission. If you are a teacher or doctor or lawyer or maintenance man, it should be easy to see your job in this vein. Sometimes our jobs finance our mission. Either way, our families should be on mission, not in tension with it. And when our family is on mission, it is the most powerful force in all the world.

Winning Beautifully with Our Businesses

Running a business and following Christ can be tenuous. What works well in the business world often stands in tension with the way of Christ. And in this area, we again usually see two alternatives. One is to get out of the business world altogether. The other is to endorse business methods in name of Christ. If it works, we say it must be godly.

But maybe neither the pacifists nor the pragmatists have it right. Maybe there are ways to do business that get us off the ladder and onto the elevator and make a profit at the same time. Maybe what the business world needs most is not Christians to abandon it or Christians to abuse it but instead Christians who imagine systems that change the world by changing the way everything is run.

Two models come to mind when I start to imagine what these kinds of systems look like. The first is a company called Toms Shoes, which was started by Blake Mycoskie. Blake and his wife were in Argentina on vacation when they found their hearts stirred and moved by two things — the Argentine style of shoe, and how many kids there didn't have shoes at all. Blake came back from this trip inspired by both of these things.

So Blake started a shoe company — but one that was a different kind of company. He used the Argentine style of shoe with an American twist to make a product he thought was stylish. But his missional strategy was to give away a pair of shoes to someone in need for every pair of shoes that he sold. And he did. Blake gave away 10,000 pairs of shoes before his company even became profitable. Now, years later, his company is both making money and helping the world.

Blake's style of business started a shoe company and put shoes on lot of kids' feet, and it is changing the way business is done. Cause marketing is now a strategy almost every company uses. And while I must admit that many businesses are now exploiting this tactic, other companies are actually following Blake's lead and doing lots of good in the world.

The second company doing business beautifully is Chick-fil-A. Referred to by some as "the Christian Chicken," Chick-fil-A runs its fast-food business differently on purpose. For one, Chick-fil-A isn't open on Sunday, and yet it still outperforms almost every other restaurant chain. Giving all of its employees a Sabbath rest, it turns out, pays off in multiple ways. But this is just one of the ways that Chick-fil-A takes care of its employees and changes the world. The way that Chick-fil-A trains its employees to treat customers is not just efficient but virtuous. And inserting virtue in a fast food restaurant is a missional task. Chick-fil-A has also started and funded the WinShape Foundation to help people make beauty out of brokenness in lots of different ways in the world. Chick-fil-A is a business not just making change but changing the world.

Each of these companies shows us just how powerful the combination of Christian mentality and economic reality can be. This was also true in the New Testament. For example, throughout Paul's ministry we find mentions of Priscilla and Aquila. These Christ-followers financed the Christian mission in the world. In fact, Paul himself was a successful man. It is not a sin to make money. But making money is not a big enough goal for any Christian business. We must create business structures that value people. We must create competition not with others but for others. And we must find ways to win in such a way that when we win, the least of these win with us.

Winning Beautifully with Our Leadership
The final place that I would like to consider what it might look like to win

beautifully today is in the area of leadership. Leadership is a buzzword both in the world and in the church. But I think it has also become one of the most abused positions in our lives. Too often, authority is synonymous with abuse. Power too often correlates with corruption. As the saying goes, absolute power corrupts absolutely.

Some people abuse power and authority on purpose. They want power as a means of passing on the abuse that was passed on to them. However, many others fall into the abuse of power by accident. It's not that they want to abuse others with their position; it's just that leadership on the ladder assumes it. As a result, when we find ourselves in positions of leadership on the ladder, we abuse that power not because we want to but because we don't know any other way.

I believe most of this abuse stems from one unquestioned assumption. When we are good at leading in one area, people assume that we are good in leading at every area. As a result, when most people start leading, they stop following. Oblivious to some of our blind spots and doing our best to cover up others, we protect our power by using our power to overpower those around us. We believe that leading at one thing means we should lead at everything. This is a lie, but too often we buy into it, and so we abuse others in the process.

Leading beautifully means understanding leadership differently. It means finding ways to follow as much as, if not more than, we lead. It means creating organizations where people have both places they lead and places they learn to submit their leadership to others. It means continuing to learn as much as we teach and empowering people with our position rather than overpowering people with our priority.

One way that we have tried to lead differently at Wayfarer is leading by collaboration. Our organization is led by not one but three positions. These positions are modeled after the Old Testament offices of prophet, priest, and king. Because Jesus was the only one to fulfill all of these offices, and none of us is Jesus, we have chosen three people to lead and follow in the way of Jesus together.

We refer to the prophet position as Lead Strategist, and this person leads our organization in visioneering and hearing from God in terms of strategy. We refer to the priest position as Lead Connector, and this person leads our organization through relationships and seeks to hear from God in communion with the people. The final position is the position of king, which we refer to as Lead Processor. The king runs the country — the business, in our case — and hears from God in finance and operations. This organizational structure requires each of us as leaders to both lead and follow in our organization. Together, we provide leadership that I think models Christ well.

While this strategy of leadership has been critiqued by some, we have found it to be a helpful way of building around one mission instead of one personality. We find that making decisions together and hearing God in multiple places cuts down on our blind spots and increases humility in each of us. As each of us submits our leadership to the other two, it helps our organization follow God instead of following a person. It's not that any of us are compromising our leadership capacity. Instead, we are learning that leadership need not be a lonely endeavor. And those within the organization would testify to the way it empowers everyone.

I give this example not to say that we have arrived but to demonstrate what imagination in leadership might look like. Who says your organization has to look like everyone else's? Who says that, to lead at one thing, you have to lead at everything? We at Wayfarer may not have it all right, but we are learning every day to lead and follow and hopefully to do so in a way that helps everyone in the organization not look like us but look like Christ. I'm sure you could improve on our start. We need you to improve on it, because the world needs more of us to rethink what leadership is supposed to be.

Redefining Normal
The great pastor and theologian Helmut Thielicke, from whose writings our ministry Wayfarer derives its name, said: "There is nothing in my life that is not changed after I have learned to say 'I believe.'" I believe he was right.

Life is short. Play hard. But also play well. Winning alone is not the goal; winning beautifully is. When we win beautifully, we win with others. And when others win with us, a movement is born.

I believe the world is once again in need of movement that shakes everything at its foundation. It's not a new movement but one as old as Christ himself. It is a subversive revolution found in a secret society that sees things differently and believes everything can change. If you are a follower of Christ, you are part of this subversive revolution. This revolution starts with Christ and isn't finished until it has upended and remade everything.

So why don't we start playing to win together? You wave your towel, and I'll wave mine. By waving them together, we'll start a movement that is the combination of lots of little movements. This movement will affect school and business and family. It will change the way we lead our lives. It will refuse to believe that what has been is the only way that things can be.

So engage your imagination. Learn to dream again. Learn to win beautifully. Because as you do, less beautiful things will become broken, and more broken things will become beautiful again. Let's Redefine Normal together.

CONCLUSION

Redefining Normal

I began this book pointing to the dichotomy I sense between following Christ and fitting into the religion of Christianity. In the pages that followed, I have done my best to open a window into my own journey to become who Jesus would be if he were me. And I have invited you to do the same. Together we have heard the challenge to become part of the subversive revolution of releasing Christ back into the heart of the Christian faith. We have tried to remember what it might be to actually be the church in and for the world. We have redefined our posture toward the world and have done our best to cast vision for the kind of epic change we believe stems from the heart of God himself. And we did it all based on a fresh sense of Bible and gospel and theology.

But as much as I can invite you to become part of this revolution, at some point you will have to choose to actually take part in it. A book can only do so much. Knowing how to become a disciple and knowing what a disciple might look like still does not equal actually becoming one. To actually become disciples, each of us needs to take what we have learned and put it into action. Reading this book might be your first action step, but it cannot be your last.

I continually return in my personal journey to two verses that have gripped me from the time when I was a junior in high school. Sitting against a big oak tree on a Spring Break retreat, I read through the book of James in my personal time with God. On my first day of reading, James 1:22 hit straight between the eyes: "Be a doer of the word and not a hearer only." Later James says, "If anyone knows to do good and doesn't do it, to him it is sin." (James 4:17, KJV) In this time alone with God, God showed me clearly my tendency to hear and not do. I knew all the God stuff and could answer all the right questions, but wasn't actually doing much if any of it. And so God's Spirit stirred my soul and began to move me out of my complacency. This book is my articulation of what I have found life with Christ outside of my own complacency to look like.

My hope is that, if this book has done anything, it has stirred you to begin a journey toward something similar in your life as well. We can be sure this journey will include both success and failure. It will be at best a continual reformation.

Redefining Normal

There will always be more of God to know. There will always be more of his life to discover. Each new discovery will continue to push us to new discoveries in ourselves and the lives we choose to live. We will not solve the Equation of Resemblance one time but instead again and again in our lives. The test of our faith, then, is not whether we have arrived but whether we will continue to have courage to change.

Change occurs as we put what we learn into practice. Hearing gives way to doing, doing gives way to learning, learning gives way to relearning, and relearning to rediscovery. This is the journey to be and become and believe.

So I end our time together not by celebrating what already is but by calling out what could be. Hear this blessing as my prayer for each of us:

May the subversive revolution poured through the secret society of the kingdom of God take root in our world and begin to turn it upside down. May it cause the dry bones to once again come back to life and become a vast army. May brokenness give way to beauty and death give way to life. As this happens, may it cause each of us to change. And as we change, may it release in us the ability to change everything.

So come wind. Come Spirit. Come in breath. Fill our lungs. Give us life. And use our lives to give life to the world. Redefine Normal!

In the name of the Father and the Son and the Holy Spirit, Amen.

APPENDIX A

Bibliography

Albert C. Outler and Richard P. Heitzenrater, ed., *John Wesley's Sermons: An Anthology* (Nashville, Tenn., Abingdon Press, 1991).

Brian D. McLaren, *The Secret Message of Jesus* (Nashville, Tenn., W Publishing Group, 2005).

Brian D. McLaren and Tony Campolo, *Adventures in Missing the Point* (Grand Rapids, Mich., Zondervan, 2003).

C.S. Lewis, *Mere Christianity* (New York, Touchstone, 1996).

Dallas Willard, *The Divine Conspiracy* (San Francisco, HarperSanFrancisco, 1997).

David J. Wolpe, *Why Faith Matters* (New York, HarperCollins, 2008).

Erwin Raphael McManus, *Seizing Your Divine Moment* (Nashville, Tenn., Thomas Nelson, 2002).

Erwin Raphael McManus, *An Unstoppable Force* (Orange, Cal., Group Publishing, 2001).

Eugene H. Peterson, *A Long Obedience in the Same Direction* (Downers Grove, Ill., InterVarsity Press, 2000).

Fisher Humphreys, *Thinking About God* (New Orleans, Insight Press, 1994).

Gordon D. Fee and Douglas Stuart, *How to Read the Bible for All It's Worth* (Grand Rapids, Mich., Zondervan Publishing House, 1993).

H. Richard Niebuhr, *Christ and Culture* (New York, Harper Torchbooks, 1957).

Helmut Thielicke, *Between Heaven and Earth* (New York, Harper and Row, Publishers, 1965).

Helmut Thielicke, *The Freedom of the Christian Man* (New York, Harper and Row, Publishers, 1963).

Helmut Thielicke, *I Believe the Christian's Creed* (Philadelphia, Fortress Press, 1968).

Helmut Thielicke, *A Thielicke Trilogy* (Grand Rapids, Mich., Baker Book House, 1980).

Henri J.M. Nouwen, *The Wounded Healer* (New York, Doubleday, 1990).

J.I. Packer, *Knowing God* (Downers Grove, Ill., InterVarsity Press, 1993).

James W. Fowler, *Stages of Faith* (San Francisco, HarperSanFrancisco, 1981).

Jim Cymbala, *Fresh Wind, Fresh Fire* (Grand Rapids, Mich., Zondervan Publishing House, 1997).

John Howard Yoder, *The Politics of Jesus* (Grand Rapids, Mich., William B. Eerdman's Publishing Company, 1990).

John Ortberg, *The Life You've Always Wanted* (Grand Rapids, Mich., Zondervan, 1997).

John Ortberg, *God Is Closer Than You Think* (Grand Rapids, Mich., Zondervan, 2005).

John Piper, *Desiring God* (Sisters, Ore., Multnomah Books, 1996).

John T. McNeill, ed. *Calvin: Institutes of the Christian Religion* (Philadelphia, The Westminster Press, 1993).

Kenneth E. Bailey, *Poet & Peasant and Through Peasant Eyes* (Grand Rapids, Mich., William B. Eerdman's Publishing Company, 1999).

Os Guinness, *Fit Bodies, Fit Minds* (Grand Rapids, Mich., Hourglass Books, 1994).

Paul Tillich, *Dynamics of Faith* (New York, Harper Torchbooks, 1957).

Philip Yancey, *Disappointment with God* (Grand Rapids, Mich., Zondervan, 1992).

Philip Yancey, *Reaching for the Invisible God* (Grand Rapids, Mich., Zondervan Publishing House, 2000).

Philip Yancey, *What's So Amazing About Grace?* (Grand Rapids, Mich., Zondervan Publishing House, 1997).

R.C. Sproul, *The Holiness of God* (Wheaton, Ill., Living Books, 1993).

Richard J. Foster, *Celebration of Discipline* (San Francisco, HarperSanFrancisco, 1988).

Richard J. Foster, *Prayer* (San Francisco, HarperSanFrancisco, 1992).

Stanley J. Grenz and Roger E. Olson, ed., *Who Needs Theology?* (Downers Grove, Ill., InterVarsity Press, 1996).

Tony Campolo, *Speaking My Mind* (Nashville, Tenn., W Publishing Group, 2004).

W. Randolph Tate, *Biblical Interpretation* (Peabody, Mass., Hendrickson Publishers, 1991).

APPENDIX B

Disciples

As I referred to in chapter 10, this is a list of a few of the people whom I have the privilege to call friend. These are not just normal friendships. This is a partial list of the band of disciples with whom I am learning to follow Christ. We are just ordinary people, who together and because of each other have been up to some extraordinary things. As you read a few lines about each of my traveling companions, I hope they help you find others like them that you could travel with.

David Reichley: David Reichley is the most Christian person I know. Even though he came to Christ long after I did — I fortunately had the opportunity to lead him in that pursuit — he now often leads me. His authentic Christ-like expression of life and faith help me remember how to respond to Christ without getting pulled into Christianese. He's always good for a practical joke or snide comment on our journey, and there is no one that I would rather have in the front seat of ministry with me than David. Thankfully, I walk beside David in leading Wayfarer today.

Chris Brooks: Chris is one of the most thoughtful, creative, and funny people I have ever known. His poetic and passionate articulation of Jesus has both helped form and nuance my own. I have loved preaching and writing with Chris because he has continuously pushed me and made me better. Even more, he has made me look more like Christ. Chris is a Wayfarer who now lives in Tuscaloosa, Alabama, and leads a group of college students at The Well. Thousands have followed Christ more closely because of Chris' life and ministry.

Chad Norris: Chad and I started Wayfarer together more than ten years ago. He is a passionate communicator and follower of Christ. He also happens to be hilarious. Life has been better these last 15 years because Chad and I have walked toward Jesus together. He is the person in my life who first pushed me toward risk in following Jesus. I largely owe the Wayfarer value of Go before Know, which has come to describe me, to him. Chad too has influenced and impacted thousands toward the kingdom through his speaking, teaching, and writing. He too now has moved to a different street address at CrossRoads Community Church, but he will always be a Wayfarer.

Roger Davis: Roger Davis is the most loyal person I have ever been friends with. He has shown me the consistency and integrity of what Christ following looks like. Recently, he has shown me how to follow Christ in the midst of suffering. I have never seen anyone face some of the greatest challenges that life could throw at a person with a greater expression of authentic faith. And in the process of journeying with him, he has strengthened my faith in Christ as well. Roger is the President of Student Life. Each year countless students and adults follow Christ more devotedly because of his ministry.

Gabe Norris: Gabe Norris is Chad's brother and my friend. He is one of the most persistent people I know. No one works harder or with greater fervency. No one laughs as loudly or enjoys celebration better than Gabe. Gabe has shown me how to work hard and laugh loud as Christ follower. He now leads Connect Ministries and WinShape Camps, and each year many children and adults know Jesus better because they have heard Gabe speak and laugh.

Dan Rhodes: Dan Rhodes is my brother and my friend. He is the most thoughtful person with whom I have ever sought God. He refuses to make faith reasonable and at the same time refuses to let faith live without reason. He challenges me constantly to see the other side of the coin when it comes to how Jesus should be lived out and expressed in the world. And yes, my younger brother is now one of my favorite teachers. Dan is currently getting his doctorate in theology at Duke Divinity School. He is an associate pastor at the Emmaus Way in Durham, N.C., and he co-authored the book *Free for All* with his pastor Tim Conder. Dan also continues to impact the world in his life and teaching.

B. J. Flora: Just in case you started to think that you had to be a professional Christian to be part of this group of disciples, I wanted to include someone who ministers more through his job than most of us ministers do in our ministries. B.J. is one of the kindest and compassionate Jesus followers I know. His lawn-maintenance business, A Cut Above, is truly an expression of Christ in the world. Not only does he make the world look better, but B.J. is also using his business to show grace in the midst of ungrace both by the way he treats his employees and in the work he does for his clients. He is also one of the most generous givers I have ever been around. In this way B.J. has and continues to show me Christ.

Robert Neely: Robert Neely shows me how to be content. He is one of the most productive and servant-minded people in the world. He constantly and relentless works to make those around him better. He receives little of the acclaim due him, but if you have ever been impacted by anything that Wayfarer does, it most certainly made its way through Robert at some point. He is my editor in more ways than he knows. He strips away my baggage and rearranges my sentences not just on a page but in life. Robert is also full of faith. He moved down from Chicago to be part of Wayfarer before we knew he would join us or how much we needed him. And I follow Christ better today because he did. Robert is both an editor and designer at Wayfarer and the glue that holds us all together.

Blake Berg: Blake Berg is an artist in every sense of the word. If you like the cover and design of this book, it's because of what came from his mind. He is a communicator through art, not simply a graphic artist. Although he is soft-spoken, when he speaks his words matter more than some of us who speak for a living. Blake shows me the disturbance and inspiration that I have grown to love in Jesus in his art and life. He is our artist (as well as our graphic artist) at Wayfarer.

Jon Helms and Chad Johnson: Jon Helms and Chad Johnson show the combination of compassion, generosity, and patience that every community needs if we are going to follow Jesus together. They do it in different ways and from different life settings, but it is the same gift. Each of them is the kind of person who is genuinely interested and listens when you speak to him. Each of them always has and makes time for me in both the little and big things of life. And as they do this, they show me the quiet and patient grace and acceptance of Christ. Jon is a life coach and counselor at Miracle Hill, a non-profit center of people in life-recovery processes. Chad is a real-estate developer. Every day, Jon and Chad influence and impact both the rich and poor through what they do and who they are.

Jason Beckner and Allen Kirkland: Jason and Allen show me the disciplined life. Allen does it with his attention to detail. He shows us how much he cares in the details, and as he does, he continuously demonstrates to me how much God is involved in the details of life. Jason shows me the power of discipline with his continued commitment to excellence in all that he does. He works at all of his life with the same effort. His consistency of quality is a quality found in Christ that I hope to emulate. Jason coaches pastors and churches at a ministry called Details. Allen is a Wayfarer now with the street address of a public school. Both of them are spreading the kingdom with their work and life.

Aaron Keyes and David Walker: Aaron Keyes and David Walker exude in their music what I hope is true of my heart — an authentic hunger for the Word and presence of God manifested both in power and priority. Aaron shows me how to be a student of the Bible, and he challenges me deeply on my inner life with God. Often we have joked with each other about who is discipling who, but all kidding aside Aaron has helped me engage in worship and discipleship at the deep level of Spirit and Truth. David Walker's hunger for the kingdom, expressed in the art of music, shows me passion at its most authentic level. David's songs move people because they are an expression of the Most Moved Mover — God Himself. Both Aaron and David lead thousands of people each year in worship through music. If you don't have their albums, you need to get them right now.

Steve Cockram and Eric Pfeiffer: Steve and Eric represent the new phase of community I have stumbled into these past few months. They accepted me into their family as one of their brothers and were a constant source of invitation and challenge in my walk with Christ as I was in Pawleys Island on sabbatical. They are new friends that feel like family, and their open-hearted generosity gave me the kind of welcome that reminds me of Jesus. Steve and Eric are part of the team at 3DM, working with my mentor Mike Breen. The global 3DM movement of church reformation really is changing the world. I am glad they have welcomed us at Wayfarer to join them. They too are helping me look like Jesus.

My Favorite Companion

Combined together, all the sentences of all the paragraphs that I have written to describe my friends could not begin to describe my favorite companion. In recent days her strength and beauty have preserved my faith and inspired me to continue to dream. She is the perfect one for me to do life with. In her consistency and humility, she shows me every day how to live like Christ. We have been married now for 13 years, and every step I have taken toward Christ beside her has been my favorite. Kim Rhodes is the person I gladly call my wife. She is the better half of me, and because I have lived life with her, I now have more resemblance to Christ than I did 13 years ago. She leads our children well, and together we lead and follow each other in the way of Christ every day.

Acknowledgements

The hardest part of writing this book is not deciding who to acknowledge for their deep and lasting contribution both to this project and to my life as a whole. It is rather deciding who not to acknowledge. In some ways, this entire book is an acknowledgment that I have not lived my life nor written this book alone. This book is the collection of the real-life contributions that many people have made to my life personally and to helping others follow Christ more fully. In the chapters of the book, I have named a few of these people. In the bibliography and list of disciples in the appendices, I have listed many more. But honestly, even in these places I have cringed in my spirit because of the many people I have left unnamed. So, to the unnamed friend who has made constant and critical contribution through conversation and life-on-life companionship, I thank you for what you have done — not just for me but now for others through this book. You know who you are, and I hope you know that I know it as well. In this project, I have been but an editor combining the words, insight, and imagination you have invested in me.

From a project standpoint, there are a few people who have given their time and energy in editing, proof-reading, and conversation that deserve special recognition. Robert Neely is chief among this group. Constantly editing and re-writing my fragmented thoughts and sentences, he has spent many hours making this manuscript clear and readable. Blake Berg served as the book's art director and designed the cover art. (You can read more about it on the About the Cover Art page.) Pete Berg served as the graphic artist in charge of layout. Helen Cockram and Dan Rhodes helped clarify thought processes, illustrations, and content in the early stages. Courtney Reichley, David Reichley, and Kim Rhodes have helped proofread so that this book is the best it can be. Rebekah Lippiatt helped organize the bibliography. The Wayfarer and 3DM Team have helped me move this conversation from our heads to real life.

Again I feel like I am leaving too many people out. Know you are not forgotten. I have just run out of space to list you and so many others like you here.

So, to all those both named and unnamed who have helped in big and small ways, I say thank you. I hope you feel as though this book is your book too. And together, as we have written the words on these pages in life, I hope that I have been as good a traveling companion to you as you have been to me.

I'm always honored when people choose me to represent them through art. And as an "I'll cook your steak rare and you'll like it or get out of my restaurant" kind of artist, I especially like it when people trust me to represent them the way that I best see fit, as Dave Rhodes has with his book.

While looking over the art for Redefining Normal, I am reminded of the Dadaist attitude toward the bourgeois capitalist society of the 1920s, my own crippling desire to live a stunted life under a banner of bourgeois capitalism, and the parallels between Dada art and my own bias toward the absurd.

If you aren't familiar with Dada (you probably aren't, and that's OK), it is only my very favorite movement (or non-movement) in all of art history. In short, the Dadaists believed that the "reason and logic" of middle class European society both allowed and defined a world that they found increasingly horrifying (World War I). In protest (artists like to protest), they abandoned reason, rationalism, and capitalism (the things that led to the current climate), and embraced chaos, senselessness, and silliness. They were the Anti-Artists of a Non-Movement. It was absurd.

I like absurdity. I like when people don't know if they should take me seriously or not. I like playful sophistication. I like to think that pigs can fly. When the impossible happens and the laws of nature are turned upside down, normal isn't normal anymore. Our imaginations are forced to imagine once again, our right to think is restored, our paradigms shift, and "normal" will never be "normal" again. Sometimes reason is unreasonable.

Reason became unreasonable for me as a full-time church staff member. I encountered bourgeois consumerism at its finest, and I embraced it. It made sense to me. I don't really know if we were doing anything wrong. But that was just it — we weren't really doing anything at all. It was safe and comfortable and anything but challenging. Pigs couldn't fly — that would be ridiculous. How absurd!

Two thousand years ago, reason was unreasonable as Jesus defied the laws of nature and society and challenged the bourgeois mainstream religious elite.

How absurd!

He raised the dead and healed the sick? How absurd!

He dined with tax collectors? How absurd!

He became Reason for the unreasonable? How absurd!

He brought Heaven to earth? How absurd!

We will do even greater things? How absurd!

We can be extraordinary disciples? How absurd!

Pigs can fly? How absurd!

Or, maybe it isn't absurd at all…

Blake Berg, artist

Biography

Dave Rhodes is a clarion voice when it comes to discipleship and church. For many years as a sought-after speaker, writer, and consultant, he has challenged the status quo of prepackaged Christianity with his profound and engaging approach to life with Christ. He combines creativity and content in a dynamic presentation that has helped many not only rethink and reorient their understanding of God, but also find and follow him. Dave is the Co-Founder and Lead Strategist of Wayfarer and the Director of Learning Communities for 3DM, where he works with multiple churches and individuals on a local and international level to provide both discipleship and missional growth. He is married to Kim and is the proud father of Emma, Izzie, and Frankie.